THE
BIBLE'S
OVERLOOKED PROMISES
AND
FORGOTTEN TRUTHS

MARK C. ALVIS

ISBN: 979-8-391-63566-6

Table of Contents

Introduction

This book is my small part in contending for the faith which was once for all entrusted to the saints – and to strengthen the witness of Christ's Church to our present generation and to the generations to come – which I believe will be many.

My goal for this short volume is to bring clarity to some biblical truths that significantly affect a Christian's worldview [the way we see reality and how we believe things ought to be]. The matters I have focused on do not deal with salvation issues, but are nevertheless important because well-meaning Christian scholars and pastors are confidently teaching the opposite of what God has promised to achieve during this New Covenant Age. Thankfully there have been godly, gifted scholars in the past who did an outstanding job in letting the Bible interpret the Bible; and there are also a growing number who are doing so today.

I pray that by correctly understanding the texts of Scripture addressed in this book, the Church will begin to speak more clearly for God and thereby better exalt His greatness, the wonder of His promises, and the amazing unity of His Word. The ten chapters of this book build upon each other. Questions raised in one chapter, may very well be answered in another chapter. I have worked hard to make this volume concise and understandable. The Scriptures I quote are from the New International Version of the Bible [NIV] unless otherwise stated. There are truths and Bible references which appear more than once, but that is not troublesome to me and it is good for you. The passages of Scripture to which I refer but do not quote are written out at the end of each chapter for your convenience and hopefully benefit.

Do you know how the Bible describes a successful Great Commission?

This book will tell you.

Dedicated to Cindy, my wife of 45 years, who listened patiently to my discoveries about the Bible and proof-read my manuscript.

Also to my youngest daughter Rachael,
who found the picture on the cover of the book
and along with her husband Nate, helped to get
my manuscript into book form.

Additionally I owe a great deal of appreciation to those who gave valuable feedback on my earlier manuscripts.

A final thanks to Dr. John Walton and Dr. Martin Poenie who were instrumental in expanding my understanding of Genesis 1 – 3.

CHAPTER 1:

Genesis 1 – 3

For a proper understanding of the Bible there is no better place to begin than with the book of Genesis – which is a Greek word meaning "origins" or "beginnings". As stated in my introduction, I believe older scholarship provides helpful insights for properly understanding particular texts of Scripture, including chapters 1 through 3 of the book of beginnings. Surprisingly some of the past viewpoints of these chapters, written in a pre-scientific era, promote more harmony between the Bible and science than do the views of many Christians today.

Mark Twain famously said, "The two most important days in your life are the day you were born and the day you find out why." Genesis 1:1 declares, "In the beginning God created the heavens and the earth." That is the beginning of everything that has been created, except perhaps for angels, who are spirit beings [Job 38:4 and 7]. But Genesis 1:1 definitively started the process which resulted in you and me. The rest of Genesis 1 gives important reasons as to WHY God created mankind. To understand the why, we must start with the meaning of the Hebrew word for create, which is "bara" and is used forty-five times in the Old Testament. As professor John Walton reminds us, "bara" is an activity of God, but it does not always speak of God creating material things. For example, in Psalm 51:10 David prays, "Create in me a pure heart, O God, and renew a steadfast spirit within me." David was not asking God to create in him a new physical heart. He had sinned greatly against God by committing adultery with Bathsheba and was asking the Lord his Shepherd to put his life back into order; to create in him a renewed desire and ability to love and obey God.

Another example for this meaning of "bara" is found in Isaiah 43:1,

> "But now, this is what the LORD says – he who created you, O Jacob, he who formed you, O Israel: 'Fear not, for I have redeemed you; I have summoned you by name; you are mine.'"

When this verse speaks of Israel being "created" – it is not referring to God making the physical bodies of the Jewish people. It is speaking about God entering into a covenant relationship with the Israelites and forming them into a nation whose purpose was to be an example to the rest of the world regarding the benefits of serving the true and living God. The importance of this meaning for create will become clearer as we continue this chapter.

Let's now look at Isaiah 45:18, "He is the God who formed the earth and made it, He established it and did not create it a waste place, but formed it to be inhabited." According to Genesis 1, the primary inhabitants God had in mind were His image-bearers, whom He appointed to be the stewards over all of His earth – as seen in Genesis 1:26-27 [ESV],

"Then God said, 'Let us [the Triune God] make man in our image, after our likeness. And let them have dominion … over all the earth and over every creeping thing that creeps on the earth.' 27So God created man in his own image, in the image of God he created him; male and female he created them."

Before going any further, we need to discuss the word for "man" which appears in Genesis 1:26 and 27. The ESV study Bible states, "The Hebrew word for man [adam] is the generic term for mankind and becomes the proper name Adam." Genesis 2:7 tells us when "adam" became a proper name,

> "The LORD God formed the man [Adam] from the dust of the ground and breathed into his nostrils the breath of life, and the man [Adam] became a living being."

In I Corinthians 15:45, the Apostle Paul indicates that Adam was the first of mankind, "So it is written: 'The first man Adam became a living being', the last Adam [Christ] a life-giving spirit." Christ is the last Adam in the sense that He is the head of a new humanity who will fulfill God's promises to Abraham, which we will discuss in chapter 2. It may be that the Adam of Genesis 2:7 was the first man in the sense that he was the head of God's original humanity. But if Adam was indeed the chronological first of mankind, it would not have prevented God from immediately creating other people in His image – and perhaps with different colors of skin.

Genesis 2 and 3 reveal that Adam was chosen by God to be the head or king of mankind. That choice carried serious ramifications which are spoken of in I Corinthians 15:22, "For as in Adam all die, so in Christ all will be made alive." How did death enter into all of mankind because of Adam? It happened when he rebelled against God's command NOT to eat from the tree of the knowledge of good and evil. That sin, which resulted in Adam's immediate spiritual death, was imputed by God to all of mankind; both those who were present on the earth at the time of Adam's fall, and to all who would follow. But why do all of us have to suffer for the sin committed by one person? R.C. Sproul reminds us it is because: (1) Adam was the man God sovereignly chose to be the head of mankind; and (2) because none of us would have done any better. The imputation of the first Adam's sin falls upon all people who experience physical life, which parallels the imputation of the second Adam's righteousness upon all people who experience spiritual life through repentance and faith in Christ [I Corinthians 15:47-48]. Those who become "new creations" are citizens of Christ's kingdom and a part of His new humanity.

The conclusion that God created other people besides Adam and Eve – right from the start – provides a better answer to the question of who did Adam and Eve's children marry? They did not need to marry their brothers or sisters because there were other people on earth for them to wed [we will deal with this issue more fully in the addendum at the end of this chapter]. The understanding that there were numerous people on earth from the very beginning, also provides a better answer as to who Cain was afraid of meeting when he was banished far away from his parents and siblings, after killing his brother Abel [Genesis 4:14].

Genesis 1:28 declares that God not only <u>designed</u> mankind to take dominion over the earth, but also <u>commanded</u> us to do so,

> "And God blessed them. And God said to them, 'Be fruitful and multiply [get married and have children] and fill the earth [build civilizations that work in harmony with God and one another] and subdue it …'"

Those commands have never been rescinded. When God used the word "subdue" – He was letting mankind know that we are going to face serious challenges in order to exercise proper dominion over the earth. This is good because it should make us depend upon God for the ability to discover and wisely use the abundant resources He has placed in and upon the earth. Mankind's fall, recorded in Genesis 3, has made this command more difficult to obey. But honest, hard work, especially when it is done for God's glory, pleases God and enables proper dominion over the earth to take place. We see indications of subduing the earth even among unbelievers in Genesis 4:20-22,

> "Adah gave birth to Jabal; he was the father of those who live in tents and raise livestock. [21]His brother's name was Jubal; he was the father of all who play the harp and flute. [22]Zillah also had a son, Tubal-Cain, who forged all kinds of tools out of bronze and iron."

Many years later when Solomon became the humble king of Israel and initially followed God's commands, he worked diligently to exercise wise dominion over the earth, as we are told in I Kings 4:29-34,

"God gave Solomon wisdom and very great insight … [31]And his fame spread to all the surrounding nations. [32]He spoke three thousand proverbs and his songs numbered a thousand and five. [33]He described plant life, from the cedar of Lebanon to the hyssop that grows out of walls. He also taught about animals and birds, reptiles and fish. [34]Men of all nations came to listen to Solomon's wisdom, sent by all the kings of the world …"

Solomon understood that we must study God's creation if we are to be good stewards over it. For example, the study of bird wings is what helped form the shape of airplane wings.

In getting back to Genesis, we should also note that Adam's fall into sin was used by God to make him the first priest [someone who helps others to connect with God]. This occurred after Adam and Eve's failure to cover the guilt of their sin by means of making fig leaf garments. Because of their inability to fix themselves, God stepped in and provided substitution for their sin by means of the shed blood of animals, whose skins were then used by God to cover Adam and Eve's nakedness [Genesis 3:21].

After the fallen couple were graciously redeemed by God, they gained the responsibility to teach their children and others that only by trusting in God's provision for sin, which required the shedding of blood [Leviticus 17:11]**, could repentant people be placed back into fellowship with God.** Abel believed what Adam and Eve taught him; Cain did not [Genesis 4:1-5].

According to Augustine [A.D. 354 – A.D. 430], Adam and Eve also had a responsibility to communicate to others the content of what they were taught by God during their six days of schooling – recorded in Genesis 1. Augustine did not believe that God created the physical heavens and the earth in six twenty-four hour days. Rather he came to believe that God taught Adam and Eve about what He had <u>already created</u> during six twenty-four hour days. The content of Genesis 2 and 3 push us in the direction that it was during the six teaching days of Genesis 1 that God put His creation into an order that would fulfill His plans and purposes. <u>And the primary way God did this was by appointing mankind to be His stewards over all the earth</u>. If you are thinking that this viewpoint gives mankind an overly exalted role in God's plans, then congratulations, King David thought the same and stated so in Psalm 8:3-6 [ESV],

> "When I look at your heavens, the work of your fingers, the moon and the stars, which you have set in place, ⁴what is man that you are mindful of him, and the son of man that you care for him? [Verse 4 is an example of Hebrew poetry, which repeats the same thought in a slightly different manner] ⁵Yet you made him a little lower than the heavenly beings [or literally a little lower than God] and crowned him with glory and honor. ⁶You have given him dominion over the works of your hands; you have put all things under his feet." These were breathtaking truths for David and should be for us as well.

From where does the idea of God conducting a week long, daytime school for Adam and Eve appear? Let's review some of the indicators. In Genesis 1:3-5, we learn about God giving names to various phenomena He had created. In Genesis 1:5, Adam and Eve learned on day one that God called the light "day" and the darkness "night". Did God give names to these realities for His benefit or for mankind's benefit? It was for man's benefit. In Genesis 1:8, God called the expanse He had made, in which the birds could fly – heaven. The Hebrew people have referred to it as the "first heaven" – which Adam and Eve learned about on day two. After God gathered the waters together and made the dry land appear in Genesis 1:9-10, He called the dry land – Earth and gathered waters – Seas. Adam and Eve were taught about the dry land's purpose on day three. On day four God spoke about the sun, moon and stars. According to the Hebrew people, the "second heaven" is where the sun, moon and stars abide. The "third heaven" is the place of God's special presence [II Corinthians 12:2-4]. Day five is when God taught Adam and Eve about the multitudes of creatures He had made to dwell in the sea, which originally covered all the earth. Day six is when Adam and Eve learned more about land animals, which God gave Adam the responsibility to observe and name in Genesis 2:19. Day six is also when Adam and Eve were told of mankind's responsibility for being God's stewards over all the earth.

A strong indication that God had regularly met with Adam and Eve is found in Genesis 3:8. After the fallen pair had unsuccessfully tried to cover their nakedness with fig leaves, we read,

> "Then the man and his wife heard the sound of the LORD God as he was walking in the garden in the cool of the day [but now because of sin, Adam and Eve had a different response to that regular occurrence], and they hid from the LORD God among the trees of the garden."

If indeed God was teaching Adam and Eve about His previous physical creation, then we should not try to make all the creative activities described in Genesis 1, as having transpired in six days. A strong endorsement for this conclusion comes when we focus on the important activities listed on the sixth day and ponder if they would have realistically occurred within the daylight hours of a single day. Hang on to your seats as we review these noteworthy events: (1) After God created all the livestock, creatures that move along the ground, and wild animals, Adam was then created in God's image, numerous hours before Eve. (2) Before God created Eve, He brought Adam into the Garden of Eden and gave him instructions about how to cultivate and keep it. (3) During the time that God was teaching Adam how to care for the many kinds of plants and trees growing in the Garden, Adam was also commanded NOT to eat from the tree of the knowledge of good and evil – upon the pain of death. Does this mean that Adam would have never experienced physical death if he had not eaten of that tree? The fact that plants, animals and man were all made from the dust of the earth indicates that their physical forms were temporary and destined to return to the dust. If Adam was created with physical immortality then there was no need for the tree of life to be in the Garden of Eden. (4) According to Genesis 2:19 Adam was then given a few hours to observe and name all the livestock, beasts of the fields and birds of the air [I am getting tired just reviewing all these activities]. But Adam's work was still not done. (5) While rapidly observing and naming all the animals, Adam was to comprehend that something wasn't right about his circumstances. According to Genesis 2:18 and 20, Adam had an aloneness problem, even though he was supposedly created just a few hours earlier and had spent most of that time with the God of the universe in a garden filled with plants delightful to the sight. (6) Adam was then put into a sleep by God and from Adam's side Eve was fashioned – perhaps around 4:00 or 5:00 p.m. on Friday afternoon. (7) Adam and Eve were then commanded to be fruitful and multiply, to fill and subdue all the earth – from whose dust they had just been made [Psalm 103:14].

Here is the main point I am trying to make. The tasks that God assigned to Adam seem far too significant to hurry through at lightening speed. In speaking for myself, I required a lengthy time of adult singleness in order to properly appreciate my need for a wife, with whom I could share life and have children.

Observations of this kind prompted Augustine to conclude in his Unfinished Literal Commentary on Genesis, that the six twenty-four hour days of Genesis 1:2-31, were days of God teaching Adam and Eve about how and why He made this world into a home for mankind. Of course what is recorded in Genesis 1 is only a small sample of what God taught them. According to Augustine, after six days of schooling God ordained the seventh day to be a time of rest for Adam and Eve, so they could reflect and celebrate all that God had revealed to them. We should all agree that our omnipotent God does not get tired and need to rest – but people do. Jesus gave an important insight when He explained that the weekly Sabbath was made for man [Mark 2:27]. In other words, God created mankind to enjoy work, but also with a need to rest after six days of serving God and our fellow man. According to the traditional view of Genesis 1, Adam was only a day old and Eve was less than a day old when God ordained the Sabbath. Why did they need a day of rest? Augustine's answer is because they had just finished six days of important schooling.

Some key points regarding Augustine's view of creation are: (1) The Bible does not tell us how long ago Genesis 1:1 occurred. But millions of unbelievers now acknowledge that the universe had a beginning – as Genesis 1:1 declares. When science came to this conclusion, it was and continues to be, extremely disappointing to multitudes of people who embrace the notion that the universe has always existed in some form, without the need of a creator. (2) Nor do we know the actual amount of time God chose to spend in making the earth into a suitable home for mankind. If the six days of Genesis 1 were days of teaching and not days of God creating material things, it removes the tension of the third day, when seeds grew into mature plants and trees – that produced vegetables and fruits in a matter of hours; and the tension that this happened without the aid of the sun, which was not created until day four. This is why Thomas Aquinas [d.1274] said,

> "If the opinion regarding [six] successive creation [days] is more common, and seems superficially to be more in accord with the letter, that of St. Augustine is more conformed to reason."

For many centuries theologians have understood that God has two books through which He speaks to man. One book is His general revelation, His creation [Psalm 19:1] – and the other book is the Bible, in which God reveals truths we could not know apart from God telling us. **Both books are accurate revelations about God and His creation. If God has provided answers to when the universe began and how long God spent in making the earth into a home for mankind – neither book will contradict the other – if both are properly understood.**

Since we are discussing Augustine's final view of the six days of Genesis 1, we must not overlook what God tells us in Exodus 20:11. Please remember that Augustine was very familiar with the Fourth Commandment,

> "For in six days the LORD made the heavens and earth, the sea, and all that is in them, and rested on the seventh day; therefore the LORD blessed the seventh day and made it holy."

It is worth observing that when Moses repeats the Ten Commandments in Deuteronomy 5, there is no mention of God creating the heavens and the earth. The stated reason for ordaining the Sabbath in Deuteronomy 5, was because of God's deliverance of the Jewish people from their slavery in Egypt, where they undoubtedly worked seven days a week.

Going back to Exodus 20:11, we should ask ourselves what does the Bible mean when it says that God "made" the seventh day holy? Did that involve physical creation of any kind? No [see one of the meanings of "made" in Psalm 7:12 and II Samuel 10:19]. God "made" the seventh day holy by using it to provide rest and corporate worship for the newly formed nation of Israel. Setting aside the seventh day provided order for the whole week. In this same way, the important truths that God taught Adam and Eve during the six days of Genesis 1, helped to put this earth into a proper working order and thus can be viewed as six days of God creating [bara] or making [asah].

Another text that points us in this direction is Genesis 2:4 [ESV],

> "These are the generations of the heavens and the earth when they were created, in the **day** that the LORD God made the earth and the heavens" [emphasis is mine].

Did God create the heavens and the earth in six days [Exodus 20:11], or in one day? If these texts are speaking about God creating the physical heavens and the earth, then we have a possible contradiction. But if both texts are speaking of God "creating or making" by means of putting His creation into a proper working order, then there is no contradiction because both are true. God did spend six days teaching Adam and Eve vital truths about His physical creation, but it was on day six that God gave mankind the command to be fruitful and multiply, to fill the earth and subdue it. Only after that command was given, could it accurately be said that God's creation was put into proper working order, which resulted in God resting.

But friends we must remember that God's desired order for this world is to be achieved by mankind humbly submitting to God and then by His grace fulfilling our responsibilities of stewardship over all the earth.

Let me pause here and share a somewhat parallel thought. In I Samuel 16 we learn that God ordered Samuel to anoint a very young David to be the <u>rightful</u> king of Israel. However, it was many years later when I Chronicles 12:38 records the process God used to make David the <u>embraced</u> king of Israel,

> "All these were fighting men who volunteered to serve in the ranks. They came to Hebron fully determined to make David king over all Israel. All the rest of the Israelites were also of one mind to make David king."

God worked through people to achieve His plans for David and for Israel. We know from Scripture that the Lord Jesus is the <u>rightful</u> king over all the earth [John 1:1-3, 10]. But God is now working through Christ's followers to make Him the <u>embraced</u> King. We are God's plan A and He has no plan B. Christ's command to make disciples of all the nations is what will lead to mankind's successful dominion over all the earth.

Before finishing this chapter I want us to look closely at Adam and Eve, whom I believe were the king and queen of mankind. I trust that what I address in this addendum will help us gain a clearer understanding of what that means and what it doesn't mean.

Addendum: Four common reasons for believing that Adam and Eve were initially the only two people on earth and that all other human beings have physically descended from them. The following are explanations for why I believe this conclusion is mistaken:

(1) Genesis 3:20, "Adam named his wife Eve, because she would become the mother of all the living." The key to properly understanding

this verse is found in Genesis 3:15, when God declared to the Satan-possessed serpent, "And I will put enmity between you [Satan] and the woman [Eve], and between your offspring and hers …" Satan's offspring are all unbelievers who never repent of their sin. In John 8:44, Jesus said to people hardened in their unbelief, "You belong to your father the devil." Eve's offspring refer to all people who enter into eternal life by trusting in God's provision for their sin. Adam and Eve died spiritually the day they ate from the forbidden tree. Their dilemma could only be overcome by God, who graciously provided substitution for their sins [Genesis 3:21]. When Adam and Eve trusted in God's provision for their sin, they were spiritually reborn and made alive. When Old Testament people put their trust in God's temporary provision for sin, it was reckoned by God as trusting in Christ, God's ultimate provision for sin [Hebrews 9:15].

In Genesis 4, after unbelieving Cain [Satan's offspring – I John 3:12], killed his righteous brother Abel [believing Eve's offspring], God gave Eve another believing son – Seth, who also had a believing son – Enosh. In Genesis 4:26 we are told, "At that time men began to call on the name of the LORD." All those who did, became the offspring of Eve. Unrepentant lost people remain prisoners in Satan's domain of darkness. Only through repentance and trust in God's provision for sin, can lost people be rescued from Satan's domain of darkness and transferred into Christ's kingdom of light [Deuteronomy 1:39; Isaiah 7:16 and Matthew 19:13-14 speak about the spiritual condition of children].

(2) Acts 17:26 [NIV], "From one man he [God] made every nation of men …" This verse literally reads [NASB], "and he made from one every nation of mankind …" The King James Version, using the Textus Receptus manuscripts reads, "and hath made of one blood all nations of men …" Therefore Acts 17:26 can properly be understood as saying, "From the one blood of mankind, or from one mankind, God made every nation of men."

(3) Genesis 2:7,

> "The LORD God formed the man [Adam] from the dust of the ground and breathed into his nostrils the breath of life, and the man became a living being."

Does this verse demand that Adam was the only human being on earth until God created Eve and then later gave them children? No. I believe Genesis 1 teaches that God created numerous people [mankind]. Genesis 2-3 progresses the story by telling us that God chose Adam to be the head of mankind.

(4) Genesis 2:18, "The LORD God said, 'It is not good for the man [Adam] to be alone. I will make a helper suitable for him." Why would God say that Adam was alone if there were indeed other people on the earth? Because God had chosen Adam to be the head and king of humanity and Adam needed a wife who would be a suitable helpmeet. He needed a queen – which God provided in Eve.

Are there texts in the Bible which support the understanding that Genesis 1:26 and 27 speak of God creating numerous people – not just two? Yes.

> Proverbs 8:27-31, "I [wisdom] was there when he set the heavens in place … ³⁰I was the craftsman at his side. I was filled with delight day after day, rejoicing always in his presence, ³¹rejoicing in his whole world and having my delight in the <u>sons of men</u>" [underlining is mine]. These verses are speaking about the condition of the world before the fall of Adam and Eve.

Ecclesiastes 7:29, "This only I have found: God made mankind upright, but men have gone in search of many schemes." The traditional view is that God made only Adam and Eve upright because they were the only two people on earth. After they rebelled against God, the stain of sin came upon them and all their offspring. A reality that must be faced is: If God initially made only Adam and Eve, and commanded their children to be fruitful and multiply, then incest was compelled by God. Many Christians see no problem with that scenario. Unbelievers, on the other hand, view God-ordained incest as a serious contradiction to the ethics of the Bible and Christianity. And yet wonderful Christian scholars continue to teach that incest only became wrong after God gave Moses His written law [<u>Theistic Evolution</u>, edited by J. P. Moreland, Stephen C. Meyer, Christopher Shaw, Ann K. Gauger, and Wayne Grudem, page 811].

That assertion is discredited by Genesis 26:1-10, where we discover in verse five that Abraham knew and obeyed God's commandments, statutes and laws hundreds of years before God gave Moses His written law. This was possible because God has always had prophets, to whom and through whom He spoke [Genesis 4:26; Amos 3:7]

– Abraham being one of them [Genesis 20:7]. Another reason why people knew about God's moral law before God gave Moses His written law, is because God's laws are written on the hearts of all people by means of our God-given consciences [Romans 2:14-15]. Honest unbelievers admit they do not live up to the standards of right and wrong revealed to them by their own consciences, which are wired to God's moral law.

We see additional evidence of people knowing that incest was wrong [long before the time of Moses] by reflecting on Genesis 26:8-10. In these verses we learn that Abimelech, the king of the Philistines, looked out his window and saw Isaac "caressing" Rebekah. He immediately knew that Rebekah was not Isaac's sister, as was claimed, because men are not supposed to do with their sisters – what Isaac was doing with Rebekah. Friends, there has never been a time when incest was necessary or morally right.

Theologians have long declared that the first covenant God established with mankind was a covenant of works. People made in God's image were to be fruitful, multiply, fill the earth and subdue it. Mankind's motive for obeying these commands was to demonstrate their love and gratitude to God. Their obedience was not a means for earning salvation because none of them were lost. However, after the fall of mankind, recorded in Genesis 3, God established a covenant of grace in order to restore repentant people into fellowship with God. This Old Covenant of grace was administered in various ways until God the Son became incarnated and inaugurated the New Covenant. It is only through repentance and faith in Christ that unsaved people can enter into the glorious New Covenant – a covenant in which God's law is written anew on our minds and hearts in such a way that we desire to embrace it. When Christians live under the guidance of God's wonderful laws, by the power of the Holy Spirit, we properly demonstrate love for God and our neighbor, as we become wise stewards over this earth – for God's glory and man's good.

Scriptures referred to but not quoted:

Job 38:4 and 7, "Where were you [Job] when I laid the earth's foundation … [7]and all the angels shouted for joy?" It would seem that angels were around before God created the earth.

I Corinthians 15:47-48, "The first man was of the dust of the earth, the second man from heaven. [48]As was the earthly man, so are those who are of the earth; and as is the man from heaven, so also are those who are of heaven."

Genesis 4:14, "Today you [God] are driving me [Cain] from the land, and I will be hidden from your presence; I will be a restless wanderer on the earth, and whoever finds me will kill me."

Genesis 3:21, "The LORD God made garments of skin for Adam and his wife and clothed them."

Leviticus 17:11, "For the life of a creature is in the blood, and I have given it to you to make atonement for yourselves on the altar; it is the blood that makes atonement for one's life."

Genesis 4:1-5, "Adam lay with his wife Eve, and she became pregnant and gave birth to Cain. She said, 'With the help of the LORD I have brought forth a man.' [2]Later she gave birth to his brother Abel. Now Abel kept flocks, and Cain worked the soil.[3]In the course of time Cain brought some of the fruits of the soil as an offering to the LORD. [4]But Abel brought fat portions [which required the shedding of blood] from some of the firstborn of his flock. The LORD looked with favor on Abel and his offering, [5]but on Cain and his offering he did not look with favor."

II Corinthians 12:2-4, "I know a man in Christ who fourteen years ago was caught up to the third heaven [the first heaven is where birds fly. The second heaven is where the sun, moon and stars abide. The third heaven is the place of God's special presence]. Whether it was in the body or out of the body I do not know – God knows.[3]And I know that this man ... [4]was caught up to paradise. He heard inexpressible things, things that man is not permitted to tell."

Psalm 103:14, "for he knows how we are formed, he remembers that we are dust." Biblically speaking we are all made from the dust of the earth, not just Adam.

Mark 2:27, "Then he said to them, 'The Sabbath was made for man, not man for the Sabbath.'"

Psalm 19:1, "The heavens declare [shout] the glory of God; the skies proclaim the work of his hands."

Psalm 7:12 [NASB], "If a man does not repent, He [God] will sharpen His sword; He has bent His bow and **made** it ready" [bold print is mine].

II Samuel 10:19 [NASB], "When all the kings ... saw that they were defeated by Israel, they **made** peace with Israel and served them" [bold print is mine].

John 1:1-3, 10, "In the beginning was the Word, and the Word was with God, and the Word was God. ²He was with God in the beginning. ³Through him all things were made; without him nothing was made that has been made … ¹⁰He was in the world, and though the world was made through him, the world did not recognize him."

Hebrews 9:15 [NASB], "And for this reason [to make full atonement for sin] He [Christ] is the mediator of a new covenant, in order that since a death has taken place for the redemption of the transgressions that were committed under the first covenant, those who have been called may receive the promise of the eternal inheritance."

I John 3:12, "Do not be like Cain, who belonged to the evil one [Satan] and murdered his brother …"

Deuteronomy 1:39, "And the little ones that you said would be taken captive, your children who do not yet know good from bad – they will enter the land."

Isaiah 7:16, "But before the boy knows enough to reject the wrong and choose the right, the land of the two kings you dread will be laid waste." The lands of both Syria and the ten northern tribes of Israel were laid waste by the Assyrians in a span of ten years.

Matthew 19:13-14, "Then children were brought to him that he might lay his hands on them and pray. The disciples rebuked the people, ¹⁴but Jesus said, 'Let the little children come to me and do not hinder them, for to such belongs the kingdom of heaven.'"

Genesis 4:26, "Seth also had a son, and he named him Enosh. At that time men began to call on [proclaim] the name of the LORD."

Amos 3:7, "Surely the Sovereign LORD does nothing without revealing his plan to his servants the prophets."

Genesis 20:7, "Now return the man's [Abraham's] wife, for he is a prophet, and he will pray for you and you will live."

Romans 2:14-15 [written around A.D. 57], "Indeed, when Gentiles, who do not have the [written] law, do by nature things required by the law, they are a law for themselves, even though they do not have the law, ^{15}since they show that the requirements of the law <u>are written on their hearts, their consciences also bearing witness</u>, and their thoughts now accusing, now even defending them" [underlining is mine]. Thankfully billions of Gentiles now have the written law of God – due to the labors of missionaries.

Genesis 26:8-9, "When Isaac had been there a long time, Abimelech king of the Philistines looked down from a window and saw Isaac caressing his wife Rebekah. ^{9}So Abimelech summoned Isaac and said, 'She is really your wife! Why did you say, "She is my sister?" Isaac answered him, 'Because I thought I might lose my life on account of her.'"

CHAPTER 2:
God's Irrevocable Promises to Abraham

In the first book of the Bible, God tells mankind about His plans for this world by means of a remarkable promise made to Abraham in Genesis 12:3, "I will bless those who bless you, and whoever curses you I will curse; and all peoples on earth will be blessed through you." This is great news, but it is a little vague as to how the nations are going to be blessed through Abraham since he has been dead for about four thousand years. God gives us more clues in Genesis 13:16, when He promised Abraham, "I will make your offspring like the dust of the earth, so that if anyone could count the dust, then your offspring could be counted." Abraham was destined to be the father of myriads upon myriads of descendants.

In Genesis 22:16-18, God expands His promises to Abraham and adds an oath to it,

> "I swear by myself, declares the LORD … [17]I will surely bless you and make your descendants as numerous as the stars of the sky and the sand on the seashore. [18]Your descendants will take possession of the cities of their enemies [literally the "gate" of

their enemies], and through your offspring all nations on earth will be blessed …"

It is worth noting that Abraham's descendants will possess the "gate" of their enemies because that is where civil leaders carried out their civil responsibilities [II Samuel 19:8; Job 29:7-17; Proverbs 31:23]. I believe this promise to Abraham's descendants indicates that God's blueprint for civil government will ultimately prevail among the nations. More about this in chapter 3.

The promises of Genesis 22:16-18 are unconditional and irrevocable. God then repeats these solemn pledges to Abraham's son Isaac in Genesis 26:2-4, and to Isaac's son Jacob in Genesis 28:13-14. Over a thousand years later the prophet Micah declared his confidence that God will do what He has promised, "You will be true to Jacob, and show mercy to Abraham, as you pledged on oath to our fathers in days long ago" [Micah 7:20]. The dark circumstances of Micah's day did not weaken his certainty that God will bless all the nations of the world through the offspring of Abraham.

I have just given six references to these foundational promises and could give more, but we need to go to the New Testament in order to clarify: (1) who the descendants of Abraham are, and (2) how they will bless all the nations. The Apostle Paul provides the answers in Galatians 3:6-8 and 29,

> "Consider Abraham: 'He believed God and it was credited to him as righteousness.' 7Understand, then, that those who believe [in Christ – Abraham's most important descendant] are children of Abraham. 8The Scripture foresaw that God would justify the Gentiles by faith [in Christ], and announced the gospel in

advance to Abraham: 'All nations will be blessed through you' …
²⁹If you belong to Christ, then you are Abraham's seed, and heirs
according to the promise."

What has the Apostle Paul taught us in these verses? (1) Christians
are descendants of Abraham through faith in Christ. Because of that
truth, we also know that (2) followers of Christ will be like the stars
of heaven in number; (3) we will possess the gate of our enemies; and
(4) we will bless all the nations of the earth. How? (5) By living and
sharing the gospel and making disciples of those who believe.

Is there anything in what I have just written that is discouraging
for followers of Christ? Then why are so many Christians wringing
their hands and saying it is all going to get worse during this New
Covenant Age? Let me quote and then explain one of the primary
texts used to support this kind of pessimism. When speaking of the
way people are to enter into the blessings of God's kingdom, Jesus
gives the following definitive teaching in Matthew 7:13-14,

> "Enter through the narrow gate. For wide is the gate and broad
> is the road that leads to destruction, and many enter through
> it [literally are entering through it]. ¹⁴But small is the gate and
> narrow [literally made narrow] the road that leads to life, and
> only a few find it" [literally are finding it].

The key to properly understanding this text is to pay attention to the
verb tenses that Christ uses. When Jesus says that "many are taking"
the broad path that leads to destruction, He used the present tense,
which means that when Jesus spoke those words two thousand years

ago, most people were taking the broad path to destruction. Christ then teaches in verse fourteen that small is the gate and "made narrow" [a participle which functions as a verb] the road that leads to life. In stating this, Jesus stepped away from the present tense and used the perfect tense, which means the road to life was narrow when Christ spoke those words, and it will always be narrow. In other words, salvation will always be by grace alone, through faith alone, in Christ alone. However, immediately after Jesus stated that abiding truth, He then goes back to the present tense when He said "only a few are finding" the path of life. When Jesus uttered those words, only a few people were trusting in Him and thus becoming the true offspring of Abraham.

Friends, this passage cannot be teaching that there will always be just a few people who will follow Christ and become the offspring of Abraham – because that would contradict the promise that Abraham's descendants will be as the stars of heaven and sand of seashore in number. What Jesus declared in Matthew 7:13-14 is that the blessings of God's Kingdom, which He came to extend upon the earth, started with just a small group of followers. But He is not teaching it was going to stay that way – which is the whole point of what He explains in Matthew 13:31-32,

> "The kingdom of heaven is like a mustard seed, which a man took and planted in his field. [32]Though it is the smallest of all your garden seeds, yet when it grows, it is the largest of garden plants and becomes a tree."

What began small, grows very large, which agrees with the prophecy of Christ's incarnation recorded in Isaiah 9:6-7,

> "For to us a child is born [small beginning], to us a son is given, and the government will be on his shoulders … [7] Of the increase of his government and peace there will be no end."

God the Son became fully man, so He could be the last Adam and the head of a new humanity – a humanity that God will use to fulfill the world-wide blessings He promised to Abraham. This is precisely what the Apostle Paul declares in Romans 15:8,

> "For I tell you that Christ has become a servant of the Jews [He was born of the Jews from the lineage of Abraham] on behalf of God's truth, to confirm the promises made to the patriarchs" [Abraham, Isaac and Jacob – underlining is mine].

The person God used to pen the letter of Hebrews, lived in the darkest hour the Church has ever known. I say that because unbelieving Jews far outnumbered Christians and they thought Christ got exactly what He deserved – death by crucifixion. During this dark time Nero also came to the throne of the Roman Empire and severely persecuted Christians. And if that wasn't bad enough, almost all of Christianity was within the borders of the Roman Empire. But in spite of those grim realities, the writer of Hebrews testified that he had total and complete trust in God and in His promise to Abraham. Listen to Hebrews 6:13-17,

> "When God made his promise to Abraham, since there was no one greater for him to swear by, he swore by himself, [14]saying, 'I will

surely bless you and give you many descendants' ... [17]Because God wanted to make the unchanging nature of his purpose very clear to the heirs [followers of Christ] of what was promised [to bless all the nations through Abraham's descendants], <u>he confirmed it with an oath</u>" [underlining is mine].

Jesus said, "I will build my Church and the gates of hell will not prevail against it." It is the Church that triumphs, not the gates of hell. Do we believe Jesus?

Scriptures referred to but not quoted:

II Samuel 19:8, "So the king got up and took his seat in the gateway. When the men were told, 'The king is sitting in the gateway,' they all came before him."

Job 29:7-17, "When I [Job] went to the gate of the city and took my seat in the public square... [16]I took up the case of the stranger. [17]I broke the fangs of the wicked and snatched the victims from their teeth."

Proverbs 31:23, "Her husband is respected at the city gate, where he takes his seat among the elders of the land."

Genesis 26:2-4, "The LORD appeared to Isaac and said... [3]'Stay in this land for a while, and I will be with you and will bless you. For to you and your descendants I will give all these lands and will confirm the oath I swore to your father Abraham. [4]I will make your descendants as numerous as the stars in the sky and will give them all these lands, and through your offspring all nations on earth will be blessed.'"

Genesis 28:13-14, "I am the LORD, the God of your father Abraham and the God of Isaac. I will give you [Jacob] and your descendants the land on which you are lying. [14]Your descendants will be like the dust of the earth, and you will spread out to the west and to the east, to the north and to the south. All peoples on earth will be blessed through you and your offspring."

CHAPTER 3:

God's Blueprint for Civil Government

This is a vitally important chapter for all Christians because of the Great Commission, which is a world changing command given by the resurrected Lord Jesus instructing His followers to make disciples of all the nations [Matthew 28:18-20]. That is a colossal, overwhelming task. However, Christ's promise <u>to be with us always</u> is the guarantee that Christians will accomplish what Christ has commanded us to do [see Exodus 3:10-12; Joshua 1:6-9 for similar promises God made to Moses and Joshua]. **Therefore a key issue the Church should presently be addressing is: "What will a successful Great Commission look like?"** One of the clearest answers is found in Isaiah 2:1-4, and for emphasis repeated in Micah 4:1-4 [I will discuss the promises of these texts in chapter 10]. However, additional help in understanding the way nations are supposed to function comes from pondering God's promise to Abraham – that his descendants will possess the "gate" of their enemies. As I mentioned in chapter 2, the gate of a city is where civil leaders conducted their civil responsibilities. To possess the gate of our enemies is to transform the civil governments of our enemies into what God wants them to be. The reality that forming godly civil governments is an important aspect of making disciples of all the nations is also gleaned from what Jacob foretold concerning his son Judah's greatest descendant. Listen to what Jacob prophesied in Genesis 49:10,

> "The scepter will not depart from Judah, nor the ruler's staff from between his feet, until he [Christ] comes to whom it belongs and the obedience of the nations is his."

The King of kings has a blueprint for civil government which needs to be understood by Christians so we can be persuasive in explaining its strengths and values to those with whom we rub shoulders.

In Exodus through Deuteronomy, God laid out governing principles, which if followed, would enable the newly formed nation of Israel to become a world leader [Deuteronomy 28:1-13]. The most vital component for catapulting Israel into greatness was God's law, which in many churches is being pitted against God's grace and the gospel. **That is unfortunate because the New Testament never speaks against God's law; it speaks against the misuse of God's law [I Timothy 1:8-11; Mark 7:8].** We should all agree that none of us can earn eternal life by our ability to keep God's law. But we can all keep it well enough to live together in a peaceful and orderly way. Since the opposite of God's law is chaos, law and order are commonly paired together.

Listen to what godly Jethro, a descendant of Abraham, advised Moses to do in Exodus 18:20, "Teach them [the people of Israel] the decrees and laws, and show them the way to live and the duties they are to perform." Showing the Israelites the proper way to live would help them become a self-governed, virtuous people, which was the foundational government for the nation of Israel and for America when it was established as a constitutional republic. Communities of people who love God and are self-governed, need very little civil government – which is an institution ordained by God to protect law abiding citizens from lawbreakers [Romans 13:1-4; I Peter 2:13-14]. Because of the fallen human condition, there will always be lawbreakers and therefore a need for civil leaders to justly punish lawbreakers and thus restrain evil [evil as defined by God and not by sinful man].

In order to help civil leaders administer just punishments, God has given them civil laws, which provide guidelines for determining fair and equitable penalties for lawbreakers [the need for God's civil law is the focus of I Timothy 1:9-11]. One of God's foundational principles for justly punishing wrongdoers is: "As you have done, it will be done to you" [Obadiah 15]. For example, if a man took a sheep from his neighbor, and was caught in his crime, the stolen sheep was returned to its rightful owner and what the thief did to his neighbor was done to him. Civil leaders would take one of his sheep and give it to the neighbor he had wronged.

An eye for an eye and a tooth for a tooth corresponds to this principle of punishment. But let me quickly clarify that when the Bible speaks of an eye for an eye and a tooth for a tooth, it does not mean that eyes were gouged out or teeth extracted. What it does mean is that after a careful and thorough trial, a person who unlawfully harmed another, had to pay a fair and adequate sum of money to the person injured [Exodus 21:18-19]. However, if a man knocked out one tooth, he should not be required to pay for three teeth – even if he happened to be wealthy. Leviticus 19:15 declares,

> "You shall do no injustice in court. You shall not be partial to the poor or defer to the great [economic status is never to be a factor in determining innocence or guilt], but in righteousness shall you judge your neighbor."

Because the authority of civil leaders is delegated by God, it only makes sense that effective civil leaders should meet the qualifications God lays out for them in Exodus 18:21,

> "But select (1) <u>capable</u> men from all the people – (2) men who <u>fear God</u> [deeply respect His moral and civil law], (3) <u>trustworthy</u> men who (4) <u>hate dishonest gain</u>" [underlining is mine].

One of the worst calamities a nation can experience is to have civil leaders who do not fear God and accept bribes in order to favor people who cheat their neighbors.

The next component of God's blueprint for civil government can be easily overlooked. In Exodus 18:21-22, Jethro informs Moses to

> "… appoint them [qualified civil leaders] as officials over thousands, hundreds, fifties and tens. [22]Have them serve as judges for the people at all times [to settle disputes by thoroughly examining the evidence of the cases brought before them], but have them bring every difficult case to you [Moses]; the simple cases they can decide themselves." Moses was comparable to our Supreme Court.

Notice that in this arrangement civil leaders who had authority over hundreds, fifties and tens, were the most numerous. They were to be chosen by the people because of their character, wisdom and honesty. And they probably served without pay. Those who were officials over thousands had heavier responsibilities, which required more of their time and therefore they may have been paid [although Job and the noble wife's husband, referred to in Proverbs 31:23, could have served without pay because they were wealthy]. These godly guidelines are repeated in Deuteronomy 1:13-17, in order to emphasize their importance.

It should not escape our notice that Jethro made no reference to kings. This was not because God is against kings. We know this because one of the promises God gave to Abraham in Genesis 17:6 states, "I will make you very fruitful; I will make nations of you, and kings will come from you." Why is there no mention of kings by Jethro? I believe it was to help the Israelites learn and develop self-government, which would then help them not to overemphasize the role of a king. The pharaohs of Egypt, where the Israelites had been enslaved, were worshiped as gods. This was not to be the case for Israel. Unfortunately, the people of Israel ended up wanting a king like all the other nations – who overemphasized the role of their kings [I Samuel 8:4-5]. The primary task God outlined for the kings of Israel is recorded in Deuteronomy 17:18-20,

> "When he takes the throne of his kingdom, he is to write for himself on a scroll a copy of this law, taken from that of the priests, who are Levites. [19]It is to be with him, and he is to read

it all the days of his life so that he may learn to revere the LORD his God and follow carefully all the words of this law and these decrees [20]and not consider himself better than his brothers and turn from the law to the right or to the left" [the law is king, not the king is law].

When king David followed these requirements, even though imperfectly, it enabled him to accomplish what is recorded in II Samuel 8:15, "David reigned over all Israel, doing what was just and right for all his people" [underlining is mine]. David's kingdom was a shadow and blueprint for how nations are to function under Christ [Isaiah 9:6-7]. The kings of Israel were to serve the people. Our Lord Jesus emphasized this quality for godly leaders in Luke 22:25-26,

> "Jesus said to them, 'The kings of the Gentiles lord it over them; and those who exercise authority over them call themselves Benefactors [who arrogantly bestowed gifts to the "common" people, whom they made sure desperately needed them]. [26]But you are not to be like that. Instead, the greatest among you should be like the youngest, and the one who rules like the one who serves.'"

Another important ingredient included in God's blueprint for civil government is found in Exodus 24:3, "When Moses went and told the people all the LORD'S words and laws, they responded with one voice, 'Everything the LORD has said we will do.'" They voted in their constitution. The principle we need to discern from this verse is that civil leaders are to govern by the consent of the people. And the laws God laid out for Israel, were good for all the people [except lawbreakers]. God testified to this truth in Ezekiel 20:11, "I gave them my decrees and made known to them my laws, for the man who obeys them will live [be blessed] by them."

Let me pause and point out an unfamiliar truth in our pulpits today. According to Christ, the two greatest commandments in the Bible are: (1) "Love the Lord your God with all your heart and with all your soul and will all your mind; (2) Love your neighbor as yourself" [Matthew 22:36-40]. **An overlooked reality is that genuine love must be grounded upon the foundation of God's moral law, which is summarized by the Ten Commandments, which were written by the finger of God [Exodus 31:18; 34:1].** Jesus said in John 14:15, "If you love me, you will obey what I command." We cannot truthfully claim to love our neighbor if we steal from him, or lie about him, or have sex with his wife. When we treasure God's law, it enables us to demonstrate how genuine love for God and our neighbor behaves.

Please consider carefully the following statements about Israel's civil government and observe who said them,

> The Bible has been the Magna Carta [the Great Charter, first published in A.D. 1215] of the poor and of the oppressed. Down to modern times no State has had a constitution in which the interests of the people are so largely taken into account; and in which the duties so much more than the privileges of rulers are insisted upon – as that drawn up for Israel. And nowhere is the fundamental truth that the welfare of the State, in the long run, depends on the uprightness of the citizens. – Thomas Huxley (1825-1895)

Thomas Huxley was an agnostic, who did not believe the Bible is God's Word, because he was not sure God even existed. But as an anthropologist he had studied the constitutions of all the nations and saw that Israel's form of government was the best. What is remarkable about Huxley's conclusion is that myriads of Christians, who do believe the Bible is God's Word, have never paid attention to what the Bible says about civil government. It is painful to admit that an agnostic had more understanding about this subject than the vast majority of Christians today. This ignorance is why Christians regularly vote to increase the size and scope of civil government and grant civil leaders authority to do – what God forbids them to do.

Huxley was right, the blueprint God laid out for Israel's civil government is designed to greatly help the poor and oppressed. But hopefully, we all realize that there are various reasons for being poor – just as there are various causes for the common cold. If people are in poverty because they are being cheated out of their wages, then civil government is to come to their aid by punishing the wrongdoers and making sure they pay restitution to those they cheated. However, according to the Bible, there are people who may be poor due to – **laziness** [Proverbs 10:4], **the love of pleasure** [Proverbs 21:17], **drunkenness and gluttony** [Proverbs 23:20-21], **stinginess** [Proverbs 28:22]. When these verses are studied, we discover that poverty may actually be a God-given consequence for wrong attitudes and lifestyles. Civil leaders will not be able to correct poverty of this nature without addressing the underlying causes – a number of which are not in the job description of civil government.

Therefore God laid out plans for helping the poor which did not involve civil government. Let me list a few examples:

(1) Leviticus 25:48-49 speaks of brothers or uncles redeeming a relative who went into servitude in order to pay his debts. The fact that he was forced to work off his debts indicates that the family members did not bail him out of his troubles, which suggests that his financial problems were self-inflicted. But if the family saw good changes taking place in the life of their relative they could redeem him out of his servitude by paying off his debt. In other words, family members were an important means for helping the poor.

(2) According to Deuteronomy 26:12, every third year the people of Israel were to give an extra tithe to the Levites, who were the pastors of Israel. The people gave double tithes on the third and sixth years because every seventh year the land rested; which means crops were not planted, or trees harvested. This resulted in the Levites and priests receiving much less tithes every seventh year. But the people of Israel were also to use portions of their double tithes to aid the aliens, orphans and widows. This assistance was given in a face-to-face manner, which enabled those who were helping the poor to address underlying issues – if necessary.

(3) God also enlisted the farmers [business people] to help the poor by leaving the edges of their fields unharvested, and then allowing the able-bodied poor to come and glean in their fields [which required work – II Thessalonians 3:10].

(4) Additionally, God gave guidelines for interest free loans to be given to the poor. The loans were to be repaid if at all possible, but if they could not be repaid, then every seventh year all unpaid loans were forgiven.

Were these provisions a part of Israel's civil laws? No. And the reason we can be sure of this is because there were no civil penalties attached to them. Farmers who did not allow the poor to glean in their fields, or people who did not give interest free loans were not punished by civil leaders. **God wanted His people to develop the quality of generosity and there is no such thing as forced generosity.** If a person could not afford to give an interest free loan, with the possibility of that loan not being repaid, then he should not give the loan. If a farmer's crop suffered from a locust infestation, he may not have been able to leave the edges of his field unharvested – because he also had to feed his family.

In short – there are many facets of everyday life that are outside the parameters of civil government. For example, do civil leaders have the authority to determine if someone is coveting what belongs to his neighbor, and then to punish him for doing so? No. However, if a person steals from his neighbor, then civil leaders are to take action against the thief, even if the plundered neighbor has a lot of money. By the way, most wealthy people have earned their money. Progressive taxation [the more income you earn, the higher percentage of your money the government takes], is practiced because civil leaders are engaged in many activities God has not called them to do. An example is Welfare, which is a forceful redistribution of wealth by civil government. Listen to what Frederic Bastiat [1801-1850], a God-fearing French economist had to say about this,

"Now legal plunder can be committed in an infinite number of ways. Thus we have an infinite number of plans for organizing it … But how is legal plunder to be identified? Quite simply. See if the law takes from some persons what belongs to them and gives it to other persons to whom it doesn't belong. See if the law benefits one citizen at the expense of another by doing what the citizen himself cannot do without committing a crime. Then abolish that law without delay …"

And may I add that any proposed law that is in opposition to God's law, should never become a civil law.

If we have citizens who truly want civil government to financially help the poor, then the next time they get their tax bill, they can pay over and above what they owe and form a fund that civil leaders can use for the purpose of helping the poor. That would be a voluntary, generous way to help the poor – although not a very smart way. I say that because government bureaucracy consumes about seventy cents of every dollar earmarked for the poor.

Are there Christians and church attenders who may get upset to hear teaching on these issues? Unfortunately yes. But as pastor Adrian Rogers [1931- 2005] correctly stated,

> "It is better to be divided by truth than to be united in error. It is better to speak the truth that hurts and then heals, than falsehood that comforts and then kills. It is better to be hated for telling the truth than to be loved for telling a lie. It is better to stand alone with the truth, than to be wrong with a multitude. It is better to ultimately succeed with the truth than to temporarily succeed with a lie."

Ryan Anderson, in his book <u>Truth Overruled</u>, wrote the following irrefutable fact of life in response to the Supreme Court's decision to legalize same-sex marriage,

> "Freedom untethered from truth is freedom's worst enemy. For if there is only your truth and my truth, and neither one of us recognizes a transcendent moral standard … call it "the truth" [God's moral law] … then the only way to settle an argument is for you to impose your power on me, of for me to impose my power on you. Freedom untethered from truth … leads first to freedom's decay, and then to freedom's demise."

The following statements are some of the declared goals of the Communist Party, published in 1958. Here are examples of the changes they wanted to make in the laws and culture of the United States:

> Eliminate all laws governing obscenity by calling them "censorship" and violations of free speech and free press. Break down cultural standards of morality by promoting pornography and obscenity in books, magazines, motions pictures, radio and TV. Present homosexuality, degeneracy and promiscuity as "normal, natural, healthy". Discredit the family as an institution. Emphasize the need to raise children away from the negative influence of parents.

These goals were established to destroy individuals, families and nations as well. It is time for followers of Christ to become long term, biblical thinkers, who positively impact our culture as we adorn both God's law and the gospel by the power of the Holy Spirit. The gospel I am speaking about is not limited to how to get saved, but also instructs and inspires saved people as to how to live and promote the Lordship of Christ in every direction that life takes us. It is by faithfully doing this that Christians will successfully make disciples of all the nations.

Addendum: A common fear about God's civil laws are the many death penalties that are invoked by them. It needs to be explained in churches that the only mandatory death penalty under the Mosaic law was for pre-meditated murder with at least two witnesses [see Numbers 35:30-31]. In other death penalty crimes such as kidnaping, adultery, homosexuality, etc – God made provisions for substitute penalties [see Exodus 21:28-30 for a clear example]. If adultery always carried a mandatory death penalty, then Jesus would not have taught that adultery was grounds for divorce, because a person does not need to divorce a dead spouse [Matthew 19:8-9].

Scriptures referred to but not quoted:

Matthew 28:18-20, "Then Jesus came to them and said, 'All authority in heaven and on earth has been given to me. [19]Therefore go and make disciples of all nations [a colossal task], baptizing them in the name of the Father and of the Son and of the Holy Spirit, [20]and teaching them to obey everything I have commanded you. And surely **I am with you always**, to the very end of the age'" [bold print is mine].

Exodus 3:10-12, "So now, go. I am sending you to Pharaoh to bring my people the Israelites out of Egypt" [a colossal task]. [11]But Moses said to God, 'Who am I, that I should go to Pharaoh and bring the Israelites out of Egypt?' [12]And God said, '**I will be**

with you. And this will be the sign to you that it is I who have sent you: **When you have brought the people out of Egypt, you will worship God on this mountain'"** [bold print is mine].

Joshua 1:1-9, "After the death of Moses the servant of the LORD, the LORD said to Joshua... 6'Be strong and courageous, because you will lead these people to inherit the land I swore to their forefathers to give them [an enormous undertaking]... 9Do not be terrified; do not be discouraged, for the LORD your God **will be with you** wherever you go'" [bold print is mine].

Deuteronomy 28:1-10, "If you fully obey the LORD your God and carefully follow all his commands I give you today, the LORD your God will set you high above all the nations on earth. 2All these blessings will come upon you and accompany you if you obey the LORD your God: 3You will be blessed in the city and blessed in the country. 4The fruit of your womb will be blessed, and the crops of your land and the young of your livestock... 7The LORD will grant that the enemies who rise up against you will be defeated before you. They will come at you from one direction but flee from you in seven... 10Then all the peoples on earth will see that you are called by the name of the LORD, and they will fear you."

I Timothy 1:8-11, "We know that the law is good **if one uses it properly**. 9We also know that law [civil law which lays out fair and just penalties] is made not for the righteous but for lawbreakers and rebels, the ungodly and sinful, the unholy and irreligious; for those who kill their fathers or mothers, for murderers, 10for adulterers and perverts, for slave traders and liars and perjurers – **and for whatever else is contrary to the sound doctrine 11that conforms to the glorious gospel** of the blessed God, which he entrusted to me" [bold print is mine].

Mark 7:8, "You have let go of the commands of God and are holding on to the traditions of men."

Romans 13:3-4, "For [godly] rulers hold no terror for those who do right, but for those who do wrong. Do you want to be free from fear of the one in authority? Then do what is right and he will commend you. [4]For he is God's servant to do you good. But if you do wrong, be afraid, for he does not bear the sword for nothing. He is God's servant, an agent of wrath to bring punishment on the wrongdoer."

I Peter 2:13-14, "Submit yourselves for the Lord's sake to every authority instituted among men: whether to the king, as the supreme authority, [14]or to governors, who are sent by him to punish those who do wrong and to commend those who do right."

Exodus 21:18-19, "If men quarrel and one hits the other with a stone or with his fist and he does not die but is confined to bed, [19]the one who struck the blow will not be held responsible if the other gets up and walks around outside with his staff; however, he must pay the injured man for the loss of his time and see that he is completely healed."

Deuteronomy 1:8-17, " … 'Go in and take possession of the land that the LORD swore he would give to your fathers – to Abraham, Isaac and Jacob – and to their descendants after them.' [9]At that time I [Moses] said to you, 'You are too heavy a burden for me to carry alone … [13]Choose some wise, understanding and respected men from each of your tribes, and I will set them over you. [14]You answered me, "What you propose to do is good." [15]So I took the leading men of your tribes, wise and respected men, and appointed them to have authority over you – as commanders of thousands, of hundreds, of fifties and of tens and as tribal officials. [16]And I charged your judges at that time: Hear the disputes between your brothers and judge fairly, whether the case is between brother Israelites or between one of them and an alien. [17]Do not show partiality in judging; hear both small and great alike. Do not be afraid of any man, for judgment belongs to God. Bring me any case too hard for you, and I will hear it.'"

I Samuel 8:4-5, "So all the elders of Israel gathered together and came to Samuel at Ramah. [5]They said to him, "You are old, and your sons do not walk in your ways; now appoint a king to lead us, such as all the other nations have.""

Isaiah 9:6-7, "For to us a child is born, to us a son is given, and the government will be on his shoulders … [7]Of the increase of his government and peace there will be no end. He will reign on David's throne and over his kingdom, establishing and upholding it with justice and righteousness from that time on and forever. The zeal of the LORD Almighty will accomplish this" [underlining is mine]. David's throne was a shadow of Christ's greater throne.

Exodus 31:18, "When the LORD finished speaking to Moses on Mount Sinai, he gave him the two tablets of the Testimony, the tablets of stone inscribed by the finger of God."

Exodus 34:1, "The LORD said to Moses, 'Chisel out two stone tablets like the first ones, and I will write on them the words that were on the first tablets, which you broke.'"

Proverbs 10:4, "Lazy hands make a man poor, but diligent hands bring wealth."

Proverbs 21:17, "He who loves [unlawful] pleasure will become poor …"

Proverbs 23:20-21, "Do not join those who drink too much wine or gorge themselves on meat, [21]for drunkards and gluttons become poor, and drowsiness clothes them in rags."

Proverbs 28:22, "A stingy man is eager to get rich and is unaware that poverty awaits him."

II Thessalonians 3:10, "For even when we were with you, we gave you this rule: 'If a man will not work, he shall not eat.'"

Numbers 35:30-31, "Anyone who kills a person is to be put to death as a murderer only on the testimony of witnesses. But no one is to be put to death on the testimony of only one witness. [31]Do not accept a ransom for the life of a murderer, who deserves to die. He must surely be put to death."

Exodus 21:28-30, "If a bull gores a man or a woman to death, the bull must be stoned to death, and its meat must not be eaten [the owner was to gain no profit from that animal]. But the owner of the bull will not be held responsible. [29]If, however, the bull has had the habit of goring and the owner has been warned but has not kept it penned up and it kills a man or woman, the bull must be stoned and the owner also must be put to death. [30]However, if payment is demanded of him, he may redeem his life by paying whatever is demanded" [underlining is mine].

Matthew 19:8-9, "Jesus replied, 'Moses permitted you to divorce your wives because your hearts were hard. But it was not this way from the beginning. [9]I tell you that anyone who divorces his wife, except for marital unfaithfulness, and marries another woman commits adultery.'"

CHAPTER 4:

The Coming of the Son of Man Mark 13

By God's grace I came to know Christ at a young age, but for many years the Bible was not a very understandable book for me. So upon completion of high school, I enrolled at Biola University and then went on to Talbot Theological Seminary. All through college and seminary I was taught by godly professors that it is normally best to take the Bible literally, because if the Bible is allegorized and taken figuratively, then people can make it say whatever they want. And that has always made perfect sense to me. But there are parts of the Bible we will find confusing and even contradictory if taken in a literal, 21st century, scientific way. So I found myself in a quandary when reading certain texts of the Bible wearing my "literal only" glasses.

Matthew 24, Mark 13 and Luke 21, which all speak of a massive judgment upon Old Covenant Israel, were initially very perplexing to me because these texts seem to be describing the end of the world, even though the context is focused upon the destruction of the stone temple at Jerusalem in A.D. 70. But one day I studied a book written by a scholarly, Bible believing pastor named Marcellus Kik. He went to be with the Lord in 1965, but was highly respected and served on the staff of "Christianity Today". He gave me a better set of glasses to wear while reading the "difficult texts". When I put those glasses on, I found whole portions of God's Word that finally came into focus and made sense. The apparent contradictions disappeared, and I gained a new confidence for the great things God is going to accomplish during this New Covenant Age. Let's look at Mark 13:1-2, which establishes the context of this chapter,

> "As he [Jesus] was leaving the temple, one of his disciples said to him, 'Look Teacher! What massive stones! What magnificent buildings!' ²'Do you see all these great buildings?' replied Jesus, 'Not one stone here will be left on another; every one will be thrown down.'"

The astonished disciples then asked Jesus in Mark 13:4, "Tell us, when will these things happen? And what will be the sign that they are all about to be fulfilled?" Jesus begins by answering their second question in verses 5-8,

> "Watch out that no one deceives you. ⁶Many will come in my name, claiming, 'I am he' [the Christ], and will deceive many [the ancient historian Josephus testifies that the nation of Israel was filled with false messiahs before Jerusalem fell – Antiquities, 20.8. 5,6]. ⁷When you hear of wars and rumors of wars, do not be alarmed. Such things must happen, but the end is still to come. ⁸Nation will rise against nation, and kingdom against kingdom. There will be earthquakes in various places, and famines. These are the beginning of birth pains."

Keith A. Mathison in his book, <u>Postmillennialism: An Eschatology of Hope</u>, page 112, lists examples of wars and uprisings which occurred after Jesus spoke these words and before Jerusalem fell: Germany, Africa, Thrace, Gaul, Britain and Armenia. Rumors of war were incited by Emperor Caligula, who ruled over the Roman Empire from A.D. 37-41. He wanted to put an image of himself in the Jewish temple, which would not happen without a declaration of war by the Jews. Thankfully, Caligula was poisoned before he could carry out his plan. Rumors of wars also spread when Claudius, who ruled the Roman Empire from A.D. 41-54, ordered all Jewish people to leave the city of Rome [Acts 18:1-2].

Earthquakes were recorded in "Crete, Smyrna, Miletus, Chios, Samos, Laodicea, Hierapolis, Colossae, Campania, Rome, Judea, Pompeii, and many other locations" [Mathison, page 112]. Scripture also records a severe empire wide famine before the temple was destroyed [Acts 11:27-30; Romans 15:25-26].

What Jesus foretold in Mark 13:9-13, was fulfilled and recorded in the book of Acts. In verse 13, Jesus warned, "All men will hate you because of me ..." Luke tells us in Acts 28:22, that after the Apostle Paul was arrested and taken to Rome, the Jews of that city told Paul, "... we want to hear what your views are, for we know that people everywhere are talking against this sect."

The warnings and advice that Jesus gave in Mark 13:14-23 will be mostly covered in my next chapter on II Thessalonians. Therefore let's go to Mark 13:24-26,

"But in those days, following that distress [leading up to the fall of Jerusalem and destruction of the temple], the sun will be darkened, and the moon will not give its light; ²⁵the stars will fall from the sky, and the heavenly bodies will be shaken. ²⁶At that time men will see the Son of Man coming in clouds with great power and glory."

This always sounded like the end of the world to me, but the clear context is the fall of Jerusalem at the hands of the Romans. What does Jesus mean when He speaks of the sun and moon being darkened and the stars falling from heaven? To answer that question we must widen our search and see how the Bible itself uses this language. And when we do, we discover that it is employed numerous places in the Old Testament to speak of God's judgments upon nations carried out thousands of years ago. Let me give you a couple of examples. One is found in Ezekiel 32:7-12, where God refers to a soon coming judgment upon Egypt,

"When I snuff you out, I will cover the heavens and darken their stars; I will cover the sun with a cloud, and the moon will not give its light. ⁸All the shining lights in the heavens I will darken over you … ¹¹'For this is what the Sovereign LORD says: "The sword of the king of Babylon will come against you. ¹²I will cause your hordes to fall by the swords of mighty men – the most ruthless of all nations. They will shatter the pride of Egypt, and all her hordes will be overthrown.""

The sun, moon and stars are at times used in the Old Testament to speak of civil rulers falling from their positions of power [Daniel 8:10]. Perhaps the Bible does this because in Genesis 1:16-18, the sun was to "govern" the day and the moon and stars were to "govern" the night.

Let's also look at Isaiah 13:9-19, which foretells Babylon's judgment by God at the hands of the Medes,

> "See, the day of the LORD is coming – a cruel day, with wrath and fierce anger – to make the land ['erets] desolate and destroy the sinners within it. [10]The stars of heaven and their constellations will not show their light. The rising sun will be darkened and the moon will not give its light. [11]I will punish the world for its evil [Babylon was considered to be a world empire] ... [13]I will make the heavens tremble; and the earth ['erets] will shake from its place at the wrath of the LORD Almighty, in the day of his burning anger [sounds like the end of the world, until we read verses 17 and 19] ... [17]See, I will stir up against them the Medes ... [19]Babylon, the jewel of kingdoms, the glory of the Babylonians' pride, will be overthrown by God like Sodom and Gomorrah."

God carried out that judgment against Babylon using the army of the Medes in 539 B.C. Therefore why shouldn't Jesus speak about the sun and moon being darkened and the stars falling from heaven when apostate Israel was judged and the temple destroyed by the armies of Rome? The surprise would be if Jesus did not use this same kind of language.

But Christ says something else in Mark 13:26 which demands our attention, "And then they will see the Son of Man [one of Christ's favorite titles for Himself] coming in clouds with great power and glory." Doesn't that have to be speaking about Christ's future Second

Coming? No. Look with me at how God's judgment against Egypt is described in Isaiah 19:1-4,

> "An oracle concerning Egypt: See, the LORD rides on a swift cloud and is coming to Egypt. The idols of Egypt tremble before him, and the hearts of the Egyptians melt within them [how was this carried out?] … ⁴I will hand the Egyptians over to the power of a cruel master, and a fierce king will rule over them."

David also speaks of Jehovah God coming on a cloud in II Samuel 22:10, when he describes God's judgment upon King Saul, using the army of the Philistines, "He parted the heavens and came down; dark clouds were under his feet." However, in Mark 13:26, Jesus says that He will be the One riding on a cloud. The reason He said that is because of a truth He taught in John 5:22-23,

> "Moreover, the Father judges no one, but has entrusted all judgment to the Son, ²³that all may honor the Son just as they honor the Father."

This means that when Jesus rose from the dead and ascended to the right hand of the Father, and the apostate nation of Israel needed to be judged, it would be the ascended Lord Jesus who would carry out that judgment – using the armies of Rome [see also Psalm 110:1-6]. I am not allegorizing this passage. I am merely letting the Bible interpret the Bible. And when we do that, it prevents the Bible from contradicting itself. Let me show you what I mean as we read Mark 13:28-31. This is when Jesus answered the first question the disciples had asked concerning the time of the temple's destruction,

> "From the fig tree learn its lesson: as soon as its branch becomes tender and puts out its leaves, you know that summer is near

[engus]. [29]So also, when you see these things taking place [false messiahs, wars, earthquakes, famines], you know that he [the Son of Man] is near [engus], at the very gates [where civil leaders exercised their authority]. [30]Truly, I say to you [Peter, James, John and Andrew] this generation will not pass away until all these things take place [referring to everything Jesus said from verse 2 through verse 30]. [31]Heaven and earth will pass away, but my words will not pass away."

If Jesus had been speaking about His Second Coming and He says in Mark 13:30, that it would take place before Peter, James, John and Andrew's generation passed away, then Jesus and the Bible are wrong. And there are a host of Bible critics who point that out. Some conservative scholars try to fix this dilemma by slicing and dicing Mark 13 – so that some of it refers to the destruction of the temple and some of it refers to Christ's Second Coming. Critics rightly point out that this understanding is imposed upon the text.

Other conservative scholars teach that all of Mark 13 refers to Christ's Second Coming – and in verse 30, "this generation" is said to be an "end of the world" generation or possibly referring to the "Jewish race" as a whole. The problem is that "this generation" never has those meanings any other place in the New Testament. Let's reason together. If we insist on taking the sun and moon being darkened and the stars falling from the sky literally – even though the Old Testament uses this same kind of language to speak of national judgments carried out thousands of years ago – we are then forced to make "this generation" mean something it never means. Isn't it more reasonable to understand the sun and moon being darkened and stars falling from the sky as a nationwide judgment, the same way the Old Testament uses this language, so we can then interpret "this generation" to mean what it always means?

Am I trying to give you a new or novel slant on Mark 13? No. Fourteen hundred years ago, four Sundays of "Advent" [taken from a Latin word which means "coming"] were put on the Church calendar in order for Christians to reflect upon four different "comings of Christ" spoken of in the New Testament. Yes, you read that correctly. The first Sunday of Advent celebrated Christ's incarnation, His "coming in the flesh" to be our perfect sacrifice for sin. The second Sunday of Advent was a time to ponder and celebrate Christ's "coming for believers" at our hour of death. When we die, which is when our spirit separates from our body, Jesus promises to come and take us to the Father's house in heaven. This is the coming of Christ spoken of in John 14:1-3, which is why that passage is often used at the funerals of Christians. The third Sunday of Advent was the fall of Jerusalem in A.D. 70, which was the imminent "coming of Christ" spoken of in the New Testament. The fourth Sunday of Advent focused on the final "coming of Christ" – which we refer to today as the Second Coming. This is when Christ will bodily raise all the dead, rapture Christians who are alive, finalize eternal destinies and usher in the Eternal State [see Advent: Encyclopedia Americana, 1960 edition. Page 164, Volume 1].

Please know that we are not speaking about a salvation issue here. Good Christians disagree about how to interpret the Olivet

Discourse. But the way we view Matthew 24, Mark 13, and Luke 21 significantly affects our worldview.

Let's move on to verse 32 of Mark 13, which also helps us to properly understand this chapter, "But concerning that day or that hour [referring to the temple's destruction], no one knows, not even the angels in heaven, nor the Son, but only the Father." If we insist that Christ was speaking about His Second Coming in Mark 13, then doesn't that mean the ascended, glorified Lord Jesus continues to be in the dark about the day and hour when He will return to earth to judge the wicked and raise the dead? We must remember that at the time Jesus spoke the truths of verse 32, He was the meek and lowly Jesus. He was fully man, and yes fully God, but He only used His divine attributes as the Father directed Him. In other words, when Jesus spoke the words of verse 32, He did not know the "day" or "hour" of the temple's destruction. The Father had not revealed those details to Him and He respected the Father's decision. But God the Father did reveal to Jesus that the temple's destruction would take place before that generation passed away. And just as Jesus warned – it did.

Friends, when Christ ascended to the seat of power, at the right hand of God the Father, He stopped being the meek and lowly Jesus who limited the use of His divine attributes of omnipotence, omniscience and omnipresence. But He doesn't do that anymore; which means He now knows with certainty the day and hour of His coming to raise the dead and usher in the Eternal State.

59

What are some of the ramifications of understanding Matthew 24, Mark 13 and Luke 21 as a prophecy concerning the fall of Jerusalem? One of the major ramifications is that the imminent "coming of Christ" – when Matthew, Mark and Luke were written, was the "coming of Christ" in judgment against apostate Israel in A.D. 70. These chapters are not focused on Christ's Second Coming. The destruction of the temple was a big deal because it marked the official end of the Old Covenant Age and animal sacrifices [Hebrews 8:7-13].

I have heard it said many times that if we are to live effectively for Christ, then we must believe that His Second Coming is just about to happen. I totally disagree with that notion. Without doubt, the Lord Jesus may come to take Mark Alvis to the Father's house at any time. I may not get my next breath. That reality gives me a sense of urgency to live my life fully for Christ, by the power of the Holy Spirit. But if we live our lives thinking that the world is just about to end, then logically Christians will be short-term thinkers who do not seriously engage our culture, nor do long range planning to make disciples of all the nations.

I believe there is one original meaning for every text of Scripture, but many legitimate applications. Let me make an application for the United States from the original meaning of Mark 13. If the United States continues to thumb its nose at what God says is right and wrong, without repentance, then we can expect a "coming of Christ" in judgment, like Old Covenant Israel experienced in A.D. 70. As a matter of fact, the United States has already suffered from a "day of the Lord" and a "coming of Christ" – it's called the Civil War, which resulted in the deaths of more Americans than all the other wars we have fought – combined. Sometime pay close attention to "The Battle Hymn of the Republic" – which is speaking about the Civil War as a "coming of Christ" in judgment upon America in the 1860's. But let's also remember that Israel's judgment in A.D. 70, and our Civil War, were not the end of the world. God judges wickedness so righteousness can continue to move forward. If the United States experiences another "day of the LORD" it will not be the end of planet earth. The vast majority of Christians are now in other nations. Friends, Christianity is growing; it is only shrinking in some areas of the world.

Scriptures referred to but not quoted:

Acts 18:1-2, "After this, Paul left Athens and went to Corinth. [2]There he met a Jew named Aquila, a native of Pontus, who had recently come from Italy with his wife Priscilla, because Claudius had ordered all the Jews to leave Rome."

Acts 11:27-30, "During this time some prophets came down from Jerusalem to Antioch. [28]One of them, named Agabus, stood up and through the Spirit predicted that a severe famine would spread over the entire Roman world. (This happened during the reign of Claudius.) [29]The disciples, each according to his ability, decided to provide help for the brothers living in Judea. [30]This they did, sending their gift to the elders by Barnabas and Saul."

Romans 15:25-26, "Now, however, I am on my way to Jerusalem in the service of the saints there. ²⁶For Macedonia and Achaia were pleased to make a contribution for the poor among the saints in Jerusalem."

Mark 13:14-23, "When you see 'the abomination that causes desolation' [spoken of in Daniel 9:27 and 12:11] standing where it does not belong – let the reader understand – then let those who are in Judea flee to the mountains. ¹⁵Let no one on the roof of his house go down or enter the house to take anything out. ¹⁶Let no one in the field go back to get his cloak. ¹⁷How dreadful it will be in those days for pregnant women and nursing mothers! ¹⁸Pray that this will not take place in winter, ¹⁹because those will be days of distress unequaled from the beginning, when God created the world, until now – and never to be equaled again. ²⁰If the Lord had not cut short those days, no one would survive. But for the sake of the elect, whom he has chosen, he has shortened them. ²¹At that time if anyone says to you, 'Look, here is the Christ!' or, 'Look, there he is!' do not believe it. ²²For false Christs and false prophets will appear and perform signs and miracles to deceive the elect – if that were possible. ²³So be on your guard; I have told you everything ahead of time."

Daniel 8:10, "It [the power of Antiochus Epiphanes] grew until it reached the host of the heavens, and it threw some of the starry host down to the earth and trampled on them."

Psalm 110:1-6, "The LORD [Jehovah] says to my Lord [Adonai – at the time of Christ's ascension]: 'Sit at my right hand until I make your enemies a footstool for your feet.' ²The LORD will extend your [the ascended Christ's] mighty scepter from Zion; you will rule in the midst of your enemies … ⁵The Lord [the ascended Christ] is at your [God the Father's] right hand; he will crush kings on the day of his wrath. ⁶He will judge the nations, heaping up the dead and crushing the [evil] rulers of the whole earth." The first time the ascended Lord Jesus did this was when He judged apostate Israel in A.D. 70.

John 14:1-3, "Do not let your hearts be troubled. Trust in God; trust also in me. ²In my Father's house are many rooms [literally dwelling places]; if it were not so, I would have told you. I am going there to prepare a place for you. ³And if I go and prepare a place for you, I will come back and take you to be with me that you also may be where I am."

Hebrews 8:7-13 [written around A.D. 65], "For if there had been nothing wrong with that first covenant [the Old Covenant], no place would have been sought for another. ⁸But God found fault with the people and said: 'The time is coming, declares the Lord, when I will make a new covenant with the house of Israel and with the house of Judah' … ¹³By calling this covenant 'new,' he has made the first one obsolete; and what is obsolete and aging will soon disappear" [when the temple was destroyed in A.D. 70].

CHAPTER 5:

Christ the King
II Thessalonians 1:4 – 2:12

T
here are important reasons why I want to teach II Thessalonians 1:4 – 2:12. These two chapters of Scripture are being explained very poorly today. The mishandling of these texts has cast doubt on the inspiration of the Bible and encourages Christians to be short-term thinkers.

Let's start with the context of II Thessalonians. How did Paul know these people? He helped to lead many of them to Christ during his second missionary journey. Acts 17:1-10 tells us what happened when Paul and Silas came to Thessalonica to share the good news of Christ,

> "When they had passed through Amphipolis and Apollonia, they came to Thessalonica [in modern day Greece], where there was a Jewish synagogue [in Paul's day, 1 out of 5 people in Thessalonica were Jewish – Encyclopedia Americana, 1960 ed. Vol. 16, page 72]. ²As his custom was, Paul went into the synagogue, and on three Sabbath days he reasoned with them from the [Old Testament] Scriptures, ³explaining and proving that the Christ [Messiah] had to suffer and rise from the dead [most Rabbis of Paul's day did not understand that truth]. ⁴This Jesus I am

proclaiming to you is the Christ,' he said. [4]Some of the Jews were persuaded and joined Paul and Silas, as did a large number of God-fearing Greeks and not a few prominent women. [5]But the [unbelieving] Jews were jealous; so they rounded up some bad characters from the marketplace, formed a mob and started a riot in the city … [6]shouting: 'These men who have caused trouble all over the world [Roman Empire] have now come here … [7]They are all defying Caesar's decrees, saying that there is another king, one called Jesus.' [8]When they heard this, the crowd and the city officials were thrown into turmoil … [10]As soon as it was night, the brothers sent Paul and Silas away to Berea."

The new believers who remained at Thessalonica were severely persecuted by the unbelieving Jews of that city. In II Thessalonians 1:4, Paul states, "Therefore, among God's churches we boast about your perseverance and faith in all the persecutions and trials you are enduring." Let's now look at what Paul stated was going to happen to those who were troubling the believers at Thessalonica. Their fate is laid out in verses 5-8,

> "All this is evidence that God's judgment is right, and as a result you will be counted worthy of the kingdom of God, for which you are suffering. [6]God is just: He will pay back trouble to those who trouble you [7]and give relief to you who are troubled, and to us as well. This will happen when the Lord Jesus is revealed from heaven in blazing fire with his powerful angels. [8]He will punish those who do not know God and do not obey the gospel of our Lord Jesus" [underlining is mine].

It is very clear that Paul was not speaking about a judgment far off into the future. Therefore, if Paul was saying that he and the believers at Thessalonica were going to be given relief from their

persecutors because the Second Coming of Christ was just about to happen – then he was wrong.

It is obvious from the context of II Thessalonians 1:5-8 that the revealing of Jesus from heaven, with his angels, would be the means of judgment upon the wicked persecutors at Thessalonica almost two-thousand years ago. This is a passage where we must recognize Paul's use of Old Testament language of judgment. In order to understand this text we need to travel back to the Thessalonica of Paul's day and discover that the circumstances of the believers in that city were very similar to the circumstances of David, when he was persecuted by King Saul. Why did King Saul want to harm David? Because Saul was jealous of David [I Samuel 18:8-9], just as the unbelieving Jews in Thessalonica were jealous of Christians [Acts 17:5]. Let me quote to you God's final earthly judgment upon King Saul, recorded in I Chronicles 10:3-6,

> "The fighting grew fierce around Saul, and when the archers overtook him, they wounded him. ⁴Saul said to his armor-bearer, 'Draw your sword and run me through, or these uncircumcised fellows [Philistine soldiers] will come and abuse me.' But his armor-bearer was terrified and would not do it; so Saul took his own sword and fell on it … ⁶So Saul and his three sons died, and all his house died together."

This passage tells us that Saul committed suicide after being wounded in battle. And yet seven verses later, I Chronicles 10:13-14 declares,

> "Saul died because he was unfaithful to the LORD; he did not keep the word of the LORD and even consulted a medium for

guidance [I Samuel 28:5-7] … ¹⁴So the LORD put him to death and turned the kingdom over to David son of Jesse."

From an earthly perspective Saul committed suicide, but from a heavenly vantage point God put Saul to death. In II Samuel 22 King David was inspired by the Holy Spirit to give a fuller account of Saul's death from God's perspective. What David wrote in II Samuel 22 is repeated in Psalm 18. When the Bible repeats something, it is for emphasis, which means it is particularly important. Let's look carefully at Psalm 18:4-16,

> "The cords of death entangled me [King Saul was using the army of Israel to hunt David down and kill him]; the torrents of destruction overwhelmed me … ⁶In my distress I called to the LORD; I cried to my God for help. From his temple he heard my voice … ⁸Smoke rose from his nostrils; consuming fire came from his mouth, burning coals blazed out of it. ⁹He parted the heavens and came down; dark clouds were under his feet. ¹⁰He mounted the cherubim and flew [angels were involved in Saul's judgment] … ¹⁴He shot his arrows [God used the arrows of the Philistines] and scattered the enemies [of David] … ¹⁶He reached down from on high and took hold of me; he drew me out of deep waters" [underlining is mine].

This is not a description of the end of the world. David is describing the end of King Saul and his rule over Israel. God's judgments upon the wicked help to deliver the righteous, who often suffer at the hands of the wicked. We see this principle all through the Old Testament. In Isaiah 40:10-24, the prophet Isaiah reviews past judgments by God. Listen to how he described them,

"See, the Sovereign LORD comes with power, and his arm rules for him. See, his reward is with him, and his recompense accompanies him [wrath upon the wicked and protection for the righteous]. [11]He tends his flock like a shepherd: He gathers the lambs in his arms and carries them close to his heart … [23]He brings [wicked] princes to naught and reduces the [evil] rulers of this world to nothing … [24]he blows on them and they wither, and a whirlwind sweeps them away like chaff."

Job 4:8-9 uses this same type of language,

"As I have observed, those who plow evil and those who sow trouble reap it. [9]At the breath of God they are destroyed; at the blast of his anger they perish."

Just as God the Father parted the heavens and came down in blazing fire to judge David's persecutor Saul, so the ascended Lord Jesus was about to do the same to the persecutors of Paul's day. It was King Jesus who would do this because when He came to earth as fully man and fully God, all judgment was handed over to Him. He began to exercise this authority at the time of His ascension [Psalm 2:6-12].

Friends, it is critical to understand that the New Testament was written under the shadow of a "day of the Lord" – an enormous, soon coming judgment – carried out by the ascended Lord Jesus. The persecutors of the Christians at Thessalonica were primarily unbelieving Jews. We should also understand that most of the false teachers in the Gentile churches Paul had planted all over the Roman Empire – were Jewish. Paul described these false teachers in I Timothy 1:4 as being devoted to myths and genealogies [very

Jewish]; in I Timothy 1:7 he said they wanted to be teachers of the law [again very Jewish]; in Colossians 2:16 the false teachers judged Gentile Christians for not eating Kosher and observing Jewish holy days; another group taught that male Gentile Christians had to be circumcised in order to be saved [Acts 15:1]. These Jewish false teachers were a blight upon the Gentile churches.

This changed in A.D. 66, when the unbelieving nation of Israel revolted against the Roman Empire. Jewish people immediately became public enemies of Rome and were killed by the droves. To escape death most of them fled from their homes to Jerusalem because it was heavily fortified. This was a mistake because many of them became casualties of the three warring factions within Jerusalem, or died of disease and starvation, or were put to the sword when Jerusalem finally fell to the Romans. The remnant of surviving Jews at Jerusalem were carried off to the salt mines or made a part of the slave laborers who helped build the Coliseum at Rome, which was financed by the gold plundered from the destroyed temple. This judgment, foretold by Christ in Luke 21, is what the Apostle Paul was calling for in I Corinthians 16:22 when he wrote,

> "If anyone does not love the Lord [primarily referring to people who claimed to love Christ, but were actually bent on destroying His Church] – a curse be on him. Come, O Lord" [Maranatha].

Paul was asking Christ to come and deliver the Christians of his day from their tormentors so the gospel could continue to move forward.

The writers of the New Testament spoke of this soon coming

judgment upon their enemies as "a revealing of Christ," or "a coming of Christ," or "a coming of Christ on the clouds," or "a day of the Lord." When Paul wrote II Thessalonians the major persecutors of the Church were unbelieving Jews. However, an even greater persecutor of the Church was in the wings. He was soon going to become the emperor of the Roman Empire. With this background in mind, lets read II Thessalonians 2:1-2,

> "Now concerning [Paul shifts gears and begins addressing a false rumor pertaining to] the coming of our Lord Jesus Christ and our being gathered to him [in protection], we ask you, brothers, ²not to become easily unsettled or alarmed by some prophecy, report or letter supposed to have come from us, saying that the day of the Lord has already come."

Most of my pastor friends believe the "day of the Lord" in this passage is referring to the Second Coming of Christ, which has still not occurred two thousand years later. One of the numerous reasons I do not believe Paul was referring to Christ's Second Coming is because he had already informed these same believers in I Thessalonians 4:16-17, that at Christ's Second coming all the saints who have died [going all the way back to righteous Abel] will be bodily raised from their graves, and all believers who are alive will be caught up to "meet" Christ in the air and receive their glorified bodies. The word "meet" that Paul employed was used to refer to a delegation of people who would go out from their city and "meet" a king in order to escort him into the city. If the rumored "day of the Lord" in verse 2 was Christ's Second Coming, then Paul could have easily squelched the false rumor by reminding the believers at Thessalonica that the dead had not been raised and none of them had been caught up to meet the Lord in the air.

The "day of the Lord" that was close at hand when Paul wrote I and II Thessalonians, was the coming of Christ in judgment against apostate Israel, which perfectly parallels what a "day of the Lord" meant in the Old Testament, as seen in Ezekiel 30:2-4,

> "Son of man [Ezekiel], prophesy and say: 'This is what the Sovereign LORD says: 'Wail and say, "Alas for that day!" ³For the day is near, the day of the LORD is near – a day of clouds, a time of doom for the nations. ⁴A sword will come against Egypt, and anguish will come upon Cush [a neighbor of Egypt]. When the slain fall in Egypt, her wealth will be carried away and her foundations torn down.'"

How did God judge Egypt in the days of Ezekiel? We are told in Ezekiel 30:10-11,

> "'This is what the Sovereign LORD says: 'I will put an end to the hordes of Egypt by the hand of Nebuchadnezzar king of Babylon [who ruled from 604 BC. to 562 B.C.] ¹¹He and his army – the most ruthless of nations – will be brought in to destroy the land. They will draw their swords against Egypt and fill the land with the slain.'"

After God used Babylon to judge Egypt, God then turned around [about seventy years later] and judged Babylon at the hands of the Medes. Babylon's "day of the Lord" is described in Isaiah 13:9-19 [cited and explained in chapter 4, page 55]. Friends, there are several different "days of the Lord" referred to in the Old Testament [Joel 1:15; Zephaniah 1:14-15; Zechariah 14:1-2; Malachi 4:5] which were carried out long ago.

Let's go back to II Thessalonians 2:2 and ask ourselves why the rumor had gotten started that the "day of Lord" against Israel had come? It is very simple. Paul wrote II Thessalonians around A.D. 51. Just a few years earlier the Roman Emperor Claudius had driven all the Jews out of Rome. We read about it in Acts 18:1-2,

> "After this, Paul left Athens and went to Corinth. ²There he met a Jew named Aquila, a native of Pontus, who had recently come from Italy with his wife Priscilla, because Claudius had ordered all the Jews to leave Rome" [which was about a tenth of Rome's population].

The probable reason for why Claudius did this was because of the turmoil in Rome caused by unbelieving Jews stirring up the city against the Christians. Aquila and Priscilla were Jewish Christians, but they were still considered Jews in the eyes of Rome, and therefore were forced to leave and move to Corinth. It would seem that false teachers used this time of turmoil to instruct the believers at Thessalonica that Israel's "day of the Lord" had come. One of the reasons why this false report was frightening to the believers at Thessalonica was because they were still being persecuted by the unbelieving Jews in their city. Paul had taught them that the day of the Lord would bring them relief. Where was the relief if the Edict of Claudius was the day of the Lord?

In verses 3-5 Paul reminds the Thessalonians what he had taught when he was with them in Acts 17,

> "Don't let anyone deceive you in any way, for that day [Christ's judgment upon Israel] will not come until the rebellion occurs [probably referring to when the nation of Israel would attempt to break away from the yoke of Rome. This happened in A.D. 66, which was still about fifteen years into their future] and the man of lawlessness is revealed, the man doomed to destruction [the man of lawlessness was not Claudius, but his adopted son Nero, who would soon come to the throne after Claudius was poisoned by Nero's mother]. ⁴He will oppose and will exalt himself over everything that is called God or is worshiped, so that he sets himself up in God's temple, proclaiming himself to be God. ⁵Don't you remember that when I was with you I used to tell you these things?"

Nero became the emperor of the Roman Empire in A.D. 54, at the age of 16. What does Paul mean when he says that Nero would oppose and exalt himself over everything that is called God or is worshiped? Nero was a part of Julius Caesar's lineage, and since Julius Caesar was officially deified after his assassination, so were the emperors who followed him. Rome did not care how many gods their subjects worshiped, as long as the Caesars were in the center of that mix.

What does Paul mean when he says that the man of lawlessness would set himself up [literally take a seat – kathisai] in God's temple [naos], proclaiming himself to be God? To properly answer this question, we must remember that Paul was writing about twenty years after Christ had died on the cross. What happened to the stone temple at Christ's death? It was made obsolete because after Christ's perfect sacrifice for sin there was no more need for animal sacrifices to be offered by Levitical priests. Ten days after Christ ascended into heaven, the new temple of God was formed on the earth, the Church of Jesus Christ [Acts 2]. Every other time Paul uses the word "naos" [temple], he is referring to Christians and Christian congregations [I Corinthians 3:16, 17; II Corinthians 6:16].

What I am saying is that when Paul was writing I and II Thessalonians, God's temple was not the obsolete stone temple at Jerusalem; it was the Church of Jesus Christ, which was spreading all over the Roman Empire. To "take a seat" [kathisai] in God's Church, meant that the man of lawlessness would acquire a position of authority over the Church [the same word is used in Matthew 23:2-3, with the meaning of acquiring authority]. When Nero became the Emperor of the Roman Empire, he acquired a position of authority over Christians because Roman 13:1-5 teaches that followers of Christ are to submit to governing authorities, unless they command what God forbids [Daniel 3:16-18], or forbid what God commands [Daniel 6:7-10]. We must also remember that almost all of the Church was within the Roman Empire when the New Testament was written. Let's move on to verses 6-8,

> "And now you know what is [present tense] holding him back [the man of lawlessness was alive when Paul wrote II Thessalonians], so that he may be revealed at the proper time. [7]For the secret power of lawlessness is already at work; but the one who now holds it back will continue to do so till he is taken out of the way [in Daniel 12, the angel Michael is called the prince of the nation of Israel. One of Michael's jobs was to protect Israel from her

enemies. It was probably when Michael withdrew his protection that the Israelites revolted against Rome and sealed their doom]. [8]And then the lawless one will be revealed, whom the Lord Jesus will overthrow with the breath of his mouth and destroy by the splendor of his coming."

This is exactly what God the Father did to King Saul and other wicked people in Old Testament times [Job 4:8-9]. But before Christ put Nero to death, He used him to give the command for Israel's revolt to be crushed. That order led to the destruction of the stone temple at Jerusalem, which marked the official end of the Old Covenant Age.

Question: How did King Saul die? He committed suicide. But in II Samuel 22:10-16, David describes Saul's death as God parting the heavens, coming down and destroying Saul with a blast of breath. King Jesus did the same to Nero, who committed suicide in June of A.D. 68. His death caused civil war to erupt in the Roman Empire. This time of turmoil for Israel and Rome gave a greatly needed reprieve for the Church, so it could continue its mission. If the ascended Lord Jesus could put an end to mighty Nero with a blast of breath, can He not also take care of the enemies of God's people today? Let's finish by reading verses 9-12,

> "The coming of the lawless one will be in accordance with the work of Satan displayed in all kinds of counterfeit miracles, signs and wonders, [10]and in every sort of evil that deceives those who are perishing. They perish because they refused to love the truth and so be saved. [11]For this reason God sends them a powerful delusion so that they will believe the lie [that man can be a god] [12]and so that all will be condemned who have not believed the

truth but have delighted in wickedness."

When Paul wrote II Thessalonians, there were temples, altars and priests who fostered emperor worship all over the Roman Empire. In these temples the priests placed images of false gods and of the Caesars. To impress people with the power of the Caesars the priests would make the images speak by means of ventriloquism, pulleys and magical materials [Grant Osborne, <u>Revelation</u> pp 515-516].

Let me clarify that the "man of lawlessness" in II Thessalonians 2, is NOT the same as the "antichrist" mentioned in I John 2:18-19. Listen carefully to what the Apostle John says about antichrists,

> "Children, it is the last hour [of the Old Covenant Age], and as you have heard that antichrist is coming, so now many antichrists have come. Therefore we know that it is the last hour. [19]They [the antichrists] went out from us, but they were not of us; for if they had been of us, they would have continued with us. But they went out, that it might become plain that they all are not of us."

The antichrists that John was speaking of were people who had professed faith in Christ but were actually opposed to Christ – and eventually showed their true colors by walking away from the local churches to which they had attached themselves. False prophets and antichrists are synonymous, and Jesus warned that many would appear before the temple was destroyed [Matthew 24:11]. Nero Caesar was the New Testament "man of lawlessness" and he never made a claim to be a follower of Christ. He actually became a great persecutor of those who did.

Let's close this discussion of II Thessalonians 1 and 2 by stating clearly that the Second Coming of Christ to raise the dead and gather His completed Bride is the great hope of the Church. That event is when perfection will be established. But the Apostle Paul is not speaking about the Second Coming of Christ in II Thessalonians 1 and 2. He is speaking about Christ's judgment upon the two great enemies of the Church in Paul's day – which were: Nero Caesar [who tradition says killed both the Apostle Paul and Peter] and unbelieving Israel. Are either of them the great enemies of the Church today? No. With a mere blast of breath, our ascended King Jesus stopped both of the Church's enemies in their tracks. The following description of the condition of the Church after the death of Nero and the fall of Jerusalem in A.D. 70, is found in The Christian History Project, Second Volume, page 16,

> "… persecutions, however, came sporadically, depending chiefly on the emperor's view of Christianity, secondarily on that of the local governor. Since Christianity was technically illegal, either authority could arrange a roundup of the Christians at any time. But the governor usually looked to Rome for direction. In the 70s and 80s, this meant Emperor Vespasian, or later to his eldest son Titus, both best known for suppressing the rebellion of the Jews and destroying their city and temple in A.D. 70. Their policy toward Christians was simplicity itself: They didn't have one. In such a hiatus, the faith spread more rapidly than ever, penetrating not only all cities but also all classes."

God's unchanging plan is to bless all the nations of the earth through Abraham's descendants – and all followers of Christ are Abraham's descendants. Therefore, we must continue to keep our eyes on Jesus and the promise that of the <u>increase</u> of His government and peace there will be no end [Isaiah 9:7].

Scriptures referred to but not quoted:

I Samuel 18:8-9, "Saul was very angry; this refrain galled him. 'They have credited David with tens of thousands,' he thought, 'but me with only thousands. What more can he get but the kingdom?' ⁹And from that time on Saul kept a jealous eye on David."

Acts 17:5, "But the Jews were jealous; so they rounded up some bad characters from the marketplace, formed a mob and started a riot in the city … "

I Samuel 28:5-7, "When Saul saw the Philistine army, he was afraid; terror filled his heart. ⁶He inquired of the LORD, but the LORD did not answer him by dreams or Urim or prophets. ⁷Saul then said to his attendants, 'Find me a woman who is a medium, so I may go and inquire of her.'"

Psalm 2:6-12, "'I have installed my King on Zion, my holy hill.' ⁷I will proclaim the decree of the LORD: He said to me, 'You are my Son; today I have become your Father [at the time of Christ's ascension, He entered into His full sonship]. ⁸Ask of me, and I will make the nations your inheritance, the ends of the earth your possession [the Great Commission is when Christ asked for the nations]. ⁹You will rule them with an iron scepter; you will dash them to pieces like pottery.' ¹⁰Therefore, you kings, be wise; be warned, you rulers of the earth. ¹¹Serve the LORD with fear and rejoice with trembling. ¹²Kiss the Son, lest he be angry and you be destroyed in your way, for his wrath can flare up in a moment."

I Timothy 1:3-4, 7, "As I [Paul] urged you [Timothy] ... command certain men not to teach false doctrines any longer ⁴nor to devote themselves to myths and endless genealogies ... ⁷They want to be teachers of the law, but they do not know what they are talking about or what they so confidently affirm."

Colossians 2:16, "Therefore do not let anyone judge you by what you eat or drink, or with regard to a religious festival, a New Moon celebration or a Sabbath day."

Acts 15:1, "Some men came down from Judea to Antioch and were teaching the brothers: 'Unless you are circumcised, according to the custom taught by Moses, you cannot be saved.'"

I Thessalonians 4:16-17, "For the Lord himself will come down from heaven, with a loud command, with the voice of the archangel and with the trumpet call of God, and the dead in Christ will rise first. ¹⁷After that, we [Christians] who are still alive and are left will be caught up together with them in the clouds to meet the Lord in the air. And so we will be with the Lord forever" [underlining is mine]. Paul probably wrote this to answer the question of what happens to Christians who are alive when Christ comes to raise the dead at the end of this New Covenant Age? The "we" that Paul uses is an editorial we, which Daniel also employed in Daniel 9:4-6, when he included himself and other righteous Jews of his day – with the rebellious Jewish people who did not listen to God's commands or to God's prophets.

Joel 1:15, "Alas for that day! For the day of the LORD is near; it will come like destruction from the Almighty." God had sent a severe locust plague upon Israel, which foreshadowed greater judgment to come if they did not repent.

Zephaniah 1:14-15, "The great day of the LORD is near – near and coming quickly. Listen! The cry on the day of the LORD will be bitter, the shouting of the warrior there. [15]That day will be a day of wrath, a day of distress and anguish, a day of trouble and ruin, a day of darkness and gloom, a day of clouds and blackness." Zephaniah is referring to the God's judgment upon Judah and the surrounding nations at the hands of the Babylonians.

Zechariah 14:1-2, "A day of the LORD is coming when your plunder will be divided among you. [2]I will gather all the nations to Jerusalem to fight against it …" Referring to Israel's judgment at the hands of the Romans.

Malachi 4:5, "See, I will send you the prophet Elijah before that great and dreadful day of the LORD comes." Referring to Israel's judgment at the hands of the Romans.

I Corinthians 3:16-17, "Don't you know that you yourselves are God's temple and that God's Spirit lives in you? [17]If anyone destroys God's temple, God will destroy him; for God's temple is sacred, and you are that temple."

II Corinthians 6:16, "What agreement is there between the temple of God and idols? For we are the temple of the living God. As God has said: 'I will live with them and walk among them, and I will be their God, and they will be my people.'"

Matthew 23:2-3, "The teachers of the law and the Pharisees sit in Moses' seat. [3]So you must obey them and do everything they tell you. But do not do what they do, for they do not practice what they preach."

Daniel 3:16-18, "Shadrach, Meshach and Abednego replied to the king, 'O Nebuchadnezzar, we do not need to defend ourselves before you in this matter. [17]If we are thrown into the blazing furnace, the God we serve is able to save us from it … [18]But even if he does not, we want you to know, O king, that we will not serve your gods or worship the image of gold you have set up.'"

Daniel 6:7-10, "The royal administrators, prefects, satraps, advisers and governors have all agreed that the king should issue an edict and enforce the decree that anyone who prays to any god or man during the next thirty days, except to you, O king, shall be thrown into the lions' den ... ⁹So King Darius put the decree in writing. ¹⁰Now when Daniel learned that the decree had been published, he went home to his upstairs room where the windows opened toward Jerusalem. Three times a day he got down on his knees and prayed, giving thanks to his God, just as he had done before."

Daniel 12:1, "At that time Michael, the great prince who protects your people, will arise. There will be a time of distress such as has not happened from the beginning of nations until then. But at that time your people – everyone whose name is found written in the book – will be delivered."

Job 4:8-9, "As I have observed, those who plow evil and those who sow trouble reap it. ⁹At the breath of God they are destroyed; at the blast of his anger they perish."

Matthew 24:11, "and many false prophets [antichrists] will appear and deceive many people."

CHAPTER 6:

The Importance of Gaining the Full Counsel of God's Word

O ne of my immovable, unshakable convictions is that truth does not contradict truth. And because all of the Bible is God's Word, all of it is true. Therefore, none of the Bible contradicts itself. If I am looking at two passages of Scripture and they seem to contradict each other, then it means that I do not properly understand one or possibly both of those texts. However, I cannot properly understand both texts if they truly contradict each other.

After decades of studying the Bible I have discovered the importance of seeking the full counsel of God's Word before coming to my conclusions on a biblical issue. Failure to seek all that God has taught about a certain event or issue, can cause us to misunderstand and misrepresent God's Word. Let me give you an important example. In Genesis 1:9-10 [ESV] we read,

> "And God said, 'Let the waters under the heavens be gathered together into one place, and let the dry land appear'; and it was so. [10] God called the dry land Earth, and the waters that were gathered together he called Seas. And God saw that it was good."

The full import of these two verses cannot be understood until we see them in the light of other related texts of Scripture. When we do so, it helps us come to a more correct understanding of the flood in Noah's day, recorded in Genesis 6-9. The four texts we are about to examine are all speaking about the creative events of Genesis 1:9-10, or they are all speaking about the destructive judgment of Noah's flood. If any of the following texts are focused on the flood, then none of the others can be referring to Genesis 1:9-10. And conversely, if any are speaking of Genesis 1:9-10, then none of the others can be speaking about the flood – unless the Bible contradicts itself, or God does not keep His promises. Let's look first at Psalm 104:5-9,

> "He set the earth on its foundations [an obvious creation activity]; it can never be moved. ⁶You covered it with the deep as with a garment [the earth was initially completely covered with water – Genesis 1:2; II Peter 3:5]; the waters stood above the mountains. ⁷But at your rebuke the waters fled, at the sound of your thunder they took to flight; ⁸they flowed over the mountains, they went down into the valleys, to the place you assigned for them. ⁹You set a boundary they cannot cross; **never again will they cover the earth**" [bold print is mine].

Psalm 104:10-28 then goes on to speak more about the blessings of God's creation. According to Psalm 104:9, after God made the dry land appear, He promised that the sea will never again cover all the earth. Matthew Henry, Charles Spurgeon, Adam Clarke, Stewart Perowne, William Plumer, Jamison, Fausset and Brown, as well as the ESV and John MacAurthur study Bibles, are all united in maintaining that this text is referring to Genesis 1:9-10, when God made the dry land appear.

Jeremiah 5:22,

> "... I made the sand a boundary for the sea, an everlasting barrier it cannot cross. The waves may roll, but they cannot prevail; they may roar, but they cannot cross it."

Tidal waves never cover all the dry land of planet earth, and they quickly return to the boundaries established by God. If Jeremiah is teaching that God did not establish these boundaries until after the destructive flood of Noah's day, then it contradicts Psalm 104, which teaches that God established the boundaries of the sea during the creation events described in Genesis 1.

Job 38:4-11, also speaks of events God performed during creation. Listen to the questions God directs to a very angry, disillusioned Job,

> "Were you there when I laid the earth's foundations? Tell me, if you understand. 5Who marked off its dimensions? Surely you know! Who stretched a measuring line across it? 6On what were its footings set, or who laid its cornerstone – 7while the morning stars sang together and all the angels shouted for joy? 8Who shut up the sea behind doors when it burst forth from the womb, 9when I made the clouds its garment and wrapped it in thick darkness, 10when I fixed limits for it and set its doors and bars in place, 11when I said, 'This far you may come and no farther; here is where your proud waves halt'?" This too is referring to the creation events described in Genesis 1.

Proverbs 8:27-31, also refers to creation events which occurred before the fall of mankind,

"I [wisdom] was there when he set the heavens in place, when he marked out the horizon on the face of the deep, [28]when he established the clouds above and fixed securely the fountains of the deep, [29]when he gave the sea its boundary so the waters would not overstep his command, and when he marked out the foundations of the earth. [30]Then I was the craftsman at his side. I was filled with delight day after day, rejoicing always in his presence, [31]rejoicing in his whole world and having my delight in the <u>sons of men</u>" [underlining is mine].

If Proverbs 8:27-31 is speaking about God setting boundaries for the sea, after destroying all of mankind except for Noah and his family by means of a global flood, then godly wisdom was rejoicing in events which grieved God – as we are told in Genesis 6:5-6,

"The LORD saw how great man's wickedness on the earth had become, and that every inclination of the thoughts of his heart was only evil all the time. [6]The LORD was grieved that he had made man on the earth, and his heart was filled with pain."

Proverbs 8:27-31 is clearly NOT referring to the flood of Noah's day, since wisdom was rejoicing in the sons of men. Nor can the flood of Noah's day have covered all the dry land of planet earth – unless the Bible contradicts itself. And yet a global flood in Noah's day is the majority viewpoint of evangelical Christians. The fact that it contradicts God's fourfold promise is supposedly countered by the declaration that Noah's flood was the one brief exception. Friends, if God did not keep a promise He repeated four times, then we cannot trust God to keep any of His promises. This of course contradicts what the Apostle Paul wrote in Titus 1:2 [NASB], "in the hope of eternal life, which God, who cannot lie, promised long ages ago."

Another shortcoming among current students of the Bible is the failure to observe that in both the Old and New Testaments, the Hebrew and Greek words for "earth" or "world" – at times are referring to the Middle East and not to planet earth. The context of the passage determines the meanings of those words. Let's look at two examples from the Old Testament:

> Zephaniah 1:2-3 [ESV], "'I will utterly sweep away everything from the face of the earth,' declares the LORD. ³'I will sweep away man and beast; I will sweep away the birds of the heavens and the fish of the sea, and the rubble with the wicked. I will cut off mankind from the face of the earth,' declares the LORD."

This is a description of God's judgment upon the nations of the Middle East, particularly Judah – at the hands of the Babylonians [Zephaniah 1:1 and 4; Zephaniah 3:8; Jeremiah 25:8-9]. However, about seventy years after Babylon conquered the nations of the Middle East, including Judah, God then judged Babylon for her wickedness – as foretold in Jeremiah 51:49, "Babylon must fall because of Israel's slain, just as the slain in all the earth have fallen because of Babylon." Had Babylon slain people all over planet earth? No. Babylon had slaughtered and conquered people all over the Middle East. Both of these texts describe judgments which took place in the Middle East, but sound as if they are speaking of the entire global earth. That reality must not be ignored.

In the New Testament, the Roman Empire was considered to be a world empire, as was Babylon in the Old Testament, even though neither of these nations came close to covering all of planet earth. Nevertheless, listen to Luke 2:1 [ESV], "In those days a decree went out from Caesar Augustus that all the world [oikoumena] should be registered." Oikoumena is translated by the NASB as "all the inhabited earth". However, the "world" or "all the inhabited earth" in Luke 2:1 is only referring to the Roman Empire, which is why the NIV translates it "the entire Roman world".

With these grammatical realities in mind, let's look at what God says in Genesis 6:17, "I am going to bring floodwaters on the earth, to destroy all life under the heavens, every creature that has the breath of life in it. Everything on the earth." When God said that He was going to destroy all life under the heavens, doesn't that mean the entire global earth was going to be submerged under water? No, because the Bible itself uses those very words when referring to a specific region of the world – rather than the whole earth. In Deuteronomy 2:25, God told Moses, "This very day I will begin to put the terror and fear of you on all the nations under heaven" [referring to nations in the Middle East]. Acts 2:5, "Now there were staying in Jerusalem God-fearing Jews from every nation under heaven." That is referring to Jews from all over the Roman Empire. Colossians 1:23, "This is the gospel that you heard and that has been proclaimed to every creature under heaven ..." Paul wrote that around A.D. 60. He is referring to the Roman Empire. Let's continue looking at Noah's flood.

Genesis 7:18-20, "The waters rose and increased greatly on the earth [land of the Middle East], and the ark floated on the surface of the water. ¹⁹They rose greatly on the earth, and all the high mountains under the entire heavens were covered [the Hebrew word for covered is "kasah" – this same word has the meaning of drench in Malachi 2:13]. ²⁰The waters rose and covered [drenched] the mountains to a depth of more than twenty feet"

When mountains are drenched with more than twenty feet of water in a short period of time, that is a jaw-dropping event. Another very important detail appears in what Moses records concerning the resting place of the ark.

Genesis 8:4-5, "and in the seventh month, on the seventeenth day of the month, the ark came to rest on the mountains [plural] of Ararat. ⁵And the waters continued to abate until the tenth month; in the tenth month, on the first day of the month, the tops of the mountains were seen."

The same Hebrew word translated "on" the mountains of Ararat is translated "against" in I Kings 6:5, "He [Solomon] also built a structure "against" the wall of the house …" Verse 4 may very well be saying that the ark rested "against" the rocky ridge that joins the two mountains of Ararat, which are seven miles apart and located in the modern-day countries of Turkey and Armenia. The Hebrew words translated "tops of the mountains" in verse 5, are translated "top of a hill" in I Samuel 26:13 and II Kings 1:9. In other words, as the waters of the flood subsided Noah was able to see the tops of the hills below him as the ark rested at a higher elevation against the rocky ridge that joins the two mountains of Ararat [view the mountains of Ararat on your computer].

When seeking the full counsel of God's Word, I believe a more biblical case is made for a flood in Noah's day that covered the Middle East, which was the biblical world of the Old Testament. Nevertheless, I do believe the flood of Genesis 6-9 is the worst judgment God has ever sent or ever will send upon mankind because at that time the majority of people lived in the Middle East. Never has such a high percentage of the world's population been destroyed by a judgment from God – and there will never again be a judgment of that magnitude. The rainbow is a reminder of that promise. All of what we have just reviewed has important ramifications concerning how to properly interpret II Peter 3 and the book of Revelation.

Scriptures referred to but not quoted:

Genesis 1:2, "Now the earth was formless and empty, darkness was over the surface of the deep, and the Spirit of God was hovering over the waters" [modern science agrees that the earth was originally covered by water].

II Peter 3:5, "But they deliberately forget that long ago by God's word the heavens existed and the earth was formed out of water and by water."

Zephaniah 1:1 and 4, "The word of the LORD that came to Zephaniah ... ⁴'I will stretch out my hand against Judah and against all who live in Jerusalem.'"

Zephaniah 3:8, "Therefore wait for me," declares the LORD ...

"I have decided to assemble the nations, to gather the kingdoms and to pour out my wrath on them – all my fierce anger. The whole world [of the Middle East] will be consumed by the fire of my jealous anger." Zephaniah and Jeremiah were contemporaries and both spoke of the same soon coming judgment.

Jeremiah 25:8-9, "Therefore the LORD Almighty says this: 'Because you have not listened to my words, ⁹I will summon all the peoples of the north and my servant Nebuchadnezzar king of Babylon,' declares the LORD, 'and I will bring them against this land [Judah] and its inhabitants and against all the surrounding nations. I will completely destroy them and make them an object of horror and scorn, and an everlasting ruin …'" This judgment by God, carried out by the hands of the Babylonians, was never to be forgotten.

Malachi 2:13, "Another thing you do: You flood [drench] the LORD'S altar with tears. You weep and wail because he no longer pays attention to your offerings …"

I Samuel 26:13, "Then David crossed over to the other side and stood on top of the hill some distance away; there was a wide space between them."

II Kings 1:9, "Then he sent to Elijah a captain with his company of fifty men. The captain went up to Elijah, who was sitting on the top of a hill …"

CHAPTER 7

An Explanation of
II Peter 3:1-13

I n this chapter I am going to apply some of the insights we have learned about the flood in Noah's day to II Peter 3:1-13. This is appropriate because Peter himself refers to the flood in II Peter 3:6. Let's begin with verses 1-4,

> "Dear friends, this is now my second letter to you [I Peter was the previous letter]. I have written both of them as reminders to stimulate you to wholesome thinking. ²I want you to recall the words spoken in the past by the holy prophets and the command given by our Lord and Savior through your apostles. ³First of all, you must understand that in the last days scoffers will come, scoffing and following their own evil desires. ⁴They will say, 'Where is this 'coming' he promised? Ever since our fathers died, everything goes on as it has since the beginning of creation.'"

When Peter wrote this letter, the scoffers may have not yet fully shown themselves in the original churches being addressed. However, their full unveiling was not far away. We know this by paying attention to a parallel passage in Jude 17-19,

"But dear friends, remember what the apostles of our Lord Jesus Christ foretold. [18]They said to you, 'In the last times there will be scoffers who will follow their own evil desires.' [19]These are the men who divide you, who follow mere natural instincts and do not have the Spirit." The scoffers whose coming was foretold by the apostles had definitely made themselves known to the churches Jude was addressing.

We need to be clear that the "last days" and the "last times" spoken of in the two quoted passages, and in every other place they appear in the New Testament, are the last days of the Old Covenant Age, which did not come to its official end until the destruction of the temple in A.D. 70. To be sure, Jesus made the temple and its animal sacrifices obsolete when He died on the cross around A.D. 30-33, but the unbelieving Jews continued to make sacrifices at that temple until it was divinely swept away about forty years after Christ's crucifixion.

When our Lord Jesus foretold the complete destruction of the temple in Matthew 24:1-2, the disciples asked Him three questions in response [Matthew 24:3]: "Tell us," they said, "when will this happen [when will the temple be destroyed], and what will be the sign of your coming and of the end of the age?" The age they were living in when these three questions were asked was the Old Covenant Age. The New Covenant had not yet been inaugurated because Jesus had not died on the cross and risen from the dead. But even after Christ accomplished those tremendous victories, the Old Covenant Age did not immediately vanish. Listen to Hebrews 8:13, written in the mid A.D. 60's. The writer of Hebrews had just quoted Jeremiah 31:31-34, which foretold the coming of the New Covenant,

"By calling this covenant 'new,' he has made the first one obsolete [the Old Covenant order was made obsolete at the cross]; and what is obsolete and aging will soon disappear."

The temple was destroyed just a few years after Hebrews was written. Its destruction was the official termination of Old Covenant Israel, but not the end of God's plans for the Jewish people. The reason why the destruction of the stone temple was considered to be the end of the Old Covenant Age is because it forever halted God ordained animal sacrifices, offered by the Levitical Priests at a stone temple. But why would the disciples consider the destruction of the temple as a "coming of Christ"? The Apostles may have first learned about this "coming of Christ" from what Jesus taught them in Matthew 10:23,

"When you [His twelve disciples] are persecuted in one place, flee to another [Jesus did not say when "we" are persecuted – because He would not be physically present during their coming persecution]. I tell you the truth, you will not finish going through the cities of Israel before the Son of Man comes."

This was the "coming of Christ" that the New Testament portrays as imminent in the days of the Apostles. According to Matthew 10:22-23, it was a coming of Christ that would liberate Christians from their persecutors by means of severe judgment upon the wicked. Jesus again speaks of this particular "coming of Christ" in Matthew 16:27-28,

"For the Son of Man is going to come in his Father's glory with his angels [in the Old Testament, God's judgments were tangible proofs of His power, which is a tangible proof of His glory. Angels were also involved – see II Kings 6:15-17; Ezekiel 9:1-6],

95

and then he will reward each person according to what he has done [the good and the bad, just as God did in the days of Noah and Lot]. [28]I tell you the truth, some who are standing here will not taste death before they see the Son of Man coming in his kingdom" [displaying His kingly power and authority].

In John 5:22-23, Jesus declared that the Father has entrusted all judgment to the Son, that all may honor the Son just as they honor the Father. If some of the disciples were not going to die before this coming of Christ occurred – then Jesus cannot be speaking about His coming at the end of the New Covenant Age. The coming that Jesus is speaking about in Matthew 16, would be experienced by some of the disciples, but most of them would have already died [martyred] before it took place. That detail rules out the possibility that Jesus was specifically speaking about His transfiguration in Matthew 17, which took place about a week later. Why? Because none of the disciples had died during that week. Neither was there a judgment upon the wicked at the time of Christ's transfiguration. The coming of Christ referred to in Matthew 16:27-28, is His coming in judgment against Old Covenant Israel, which resulted in the destruction of the temple. Only a few of the disciples lived to see that happen.

It is this "coming of Christ" that Peter is dealing with in II Peter 3:4, "They [the scoffers] will say, 'Where is this coming he [Christ] promised? Ever since our fathers died, everything goes on as it has since the beginning of creation.'" The catastrophic judgement Jesus warned would come upon Peter's generation had not yet occurred when II Peter was written [Peter himself did not live to see it].

However, Jesus promised it would come before that generation passed away [Matthew 24:34]. The scoffers of Peter's day boasted that because it hadn't happened yet, it wasn't going to happen. Listen to Peter's reply to these scoffers in II Peter 3:5-7,

> "But they deliberately forget that long ago by God's word the heavens existed and the earth was formed out of water and by water [Genesis 1:6-10]. ⁶By these waters also the world [kosmos – see John 12:19] of that time was deluged and destroyed. ⁷By the same word [the same authority and power behind Noah's flood] the present heavens and earth are reserved for fire [judgment], being kept for the day of judgment and destruction of ungodly men."

Initially the earth was entirely covered by water, some of which was used to form the earth's atmosphere. But even after God formed the atmosphere the water which remained on the earth – covered all the earth. That changed when God made the dry land appear [spoken of in Genesis 1:9-10] and then promised that the dry land of earth would never again be completely covered by water [Psalm 104:5-9]. As we have already discussed – the flood in Noah's day covered the Middle East, where the majority of mankind lived, but not all of planet earth. Neither was the coming of Christ in II Peter 3, going to wreck havoc upon all the inhabitants of planet earth. It was primarily focused on apostate Old Covenant Israel, but also rippled out to the Roman Empire. This was the understanding of John Lightfoot [1602-1675] and John Owen [1616-1683] – two greatly gifted Bible scholars. Let's continue looking at verses 8-10,

"But do not forget this one thing, dear friends: With the Lord a day is like a thousand years, and a thousand years are like a day. [9]The Lord is not slow in keeping his promise [to judge unbelieving Israel], as some understand slowness. He is patient with you, not wanting anyone to perish, but everyone to come to repentance. [10]But the day of the Lord will come like a thief [this imagery is found in Matthew 24:42-44, which is referring to the fall of Jerusalem in A.D. 70]. The heavens will disappear with a roar, the elements [stoixeia] will be destroyed by fire and the earth and everything in it will be laid bare" [underlining is mine].

When Peter speaks about the heavens disappearing, he is borrowing from the imagery found in Isaiah 34:4, "All the stars of the heavens will be dissolved and the sky rolled up like a scroll." In that passage Isaiah was speaking of Edom's judgment at the hands of the Babylonians. Peter goes on to speak of the elements [stoixeia] being destroyed by fire. The Greek word Peter used for elements is found only four other times in the New Testament – Galatians 4:9; Colossians 2:8, 20; Hebrews 5:12. In all these other passages, stoixeia means principles, philosophies and ideologies – not land, trees and buildings. Next Peter speaks of the earth and everything in it being laid bare, which is quite similar to how David described God's judgment upon King Saul in II Samuel 22:7-16,

"In my distress I called to the LORD; I called out to my God. From his temple he heard my voice … [10]He parted the heavens and came down … [16]The valleys of the sea were exposed and the foundations of the earth laid bare at the rebuke of the LORD, at the blast of breath from his nostrils" [underlining is mine].

Against all odds, Saul's kingdom was toppled, and David's kingdom was established. Why do commentaries and study Bibles resist the notion that Christ and the New Testament writers used the same kind of language employed by Old Testament writers? Let's return to II Peter 3:11-12,

> "Since everything will be destroyed in this way [Old Covenant Israel and the Old Covenant order], what kind of people ought you to be? You ought to live holy and godly lives [12]as you look forward to the day of God and speed its coming. That day will bring about the destruction of the heavens by fire [probably referring to judgment upon Israel's civil leaders and Nero], and the elements [stoixeia – the false ideologies of the unbelieving Jews of that time] will melt in the heat."

If Peter is speaking about the end of planet earth, thousands of years into his future, how was that going to affect people who lived and died 2,000 years ago? We must understand that there really was an enormous judgment coming in Peter's day, which he described with Old Testament language. For example, Psalm 46:6 speaks of God's wrath against wicked nations in the following way, "Nations are in an uproar, kingdoms fall; he lifts his voice, the earth melts." That passage is probably describing God's judgment against Israel and her neighbors at the hands of the Assyrians. Micah 1:2-6, is without doubt speaking about that judgment,

> "Hear, O peoples, all of you, listen, O earth and all who are in it, that the Sovereign LORD may witness against you, the Lord from his holy temple. [3]Look! The LORD is coming from his dwelling place; he comes down and treads the high places of the

earth [where unbelieving Jews practiced their idolatry]. ⁴The mountains melt beneath him and the valleys split apart, like wax before the fire, like water rushing down a slope. ⁵All this is because of Jacob's transgression, because of the sins of the house of Israel … ⁶Therefore I will make Samaria [the capital city of the ten northern tribes] a heap of rubble, a place for planting vineyards. I will pour her stones into the valley and lay bare her foundations" [accomplished in 722 B.C.].

Peter is using this same kind of language to describe the end of Old Covenant Israel in A.D. 70. But please note, even though fearsome judgment was on the horizon when II Peter was written, that was NOT God's long-range plans for the peoples of the earth. The Apostle Peter goes on to say in II Peter 3:13, "But in keeping with his promise [Isaiah 65:17-25; Isaiah 66:22-23; see chapter 8] we are looking forward to a new heaven and a new earth, the home of righteousness."

Every Christian should look forward to the final advent of Christ and the ushering in of the Eternal State. Most Christians correctly view the Eternal State as synonymous with the new heaven and new earth described in Revelation 21:1-4. However, there is not just one sense in which the phrase "new heavens and new earth" is used in the Bible. When Peter was writing this letter, there were only two biblical references to the new heavens and earth – Isaiah 65 and 66. And neither one of those texts are speaking about the new heaven and new earth spoken of in Revelation 21:1-4. I say that because the new heaven and new earth that the Apostle John depicts in Revelation 21, clearly reveals that death will be no more. However, the new heavens and earth described in Isaiah 65:17-25 speaks of people living long lives but still dying.

Let me close by stating that the final advent of Christ [which we refer to as Christ's Second Coming] will not be for the purpose of burning up planet earth. That notion comes from an improper understanding of the Apostle Peter's words, which occurs when we ignore the time indicators of the text and when we refuse to see the reality that New Testament writers used Old Testament language of judgment. We must not forget God's promise to Noah and his sons recorded in Genesis 9:11-16, guaranteeing that the severity of God's judgment in Noah's day will never again be equaled. And yet the way many Christians are understanding II Peter 3 makes a judgment coming sometime in our future – worse than the flood of Noah's day. Friends, that interpretation of II Peter 3 makes the Bible contradict itself.

Martin Luther [1483-1564] once said, "If I knew Christ was coming tomorrow, I would plant a tree today." Luther understood from Scripture that Christians who are alive at the final advent of Christ will be caught up and transformed in the twinkling of an eye [I Corinthians 15:49-53]. Their mortal bodies will NOT be burned up or annihilated but transfigured into glorified bodies. Luther believed the same will be true of the present heavens and earth and therefore he wanted to see what his newly planted tree would look like on the ultimate new earth.

Addendum: Why the biblical meaning of "last days" is vitally important.

Hebrews 1:2 teaches that the incarnation of Christ occurred in the last days; not the last days of planet earth, but rather the last days of the Old Covenant Age which ended with the Old Covenant temple being destroyed in A.D. 70. John A. T. Robinson [1919-1983] in his book, <u>Redating the New Testament</u>, concluded that all of the New Testament was completed before A.D. 70, which is why the New Testament writers never speak of the temple as having already been destroyed. Another support for this conclusion appears in Acts 2:14-21, in which Peter quoted verbatim – Joel 2:28-32. However, Peter was guided by the Holy Spirit to add the words, "in the last days" – which gave the context of when this portion of Joel's prophecy would be fulfilled. Why is that significant? Because the following blessings transpired in "the last days" before the temple was destroyed, "Your sons and daughters will prophesy, your young men will see visions, your old men will dream dreams …" This is language of revelation. It was through prophecy, dreams and visions that we received our Old Testament [I Samuel 3:1; II Chronicles 32:32; Daniel 7:1; Amos 3:7]. According to Peter, God was going to give His revelation for the New Testament during "the last days" of the Old Covenant Age, which agrees with Daniel 9:24-27.

It was also during that same period of time when Joel 2:30-31 would be fulfilled,

> "I will show wonders in the heavens and on the earth, blood and fire and billows of smoke. [31]The sun will be turned to darkness and the moon to blood before the coming of the great and dreadful day of the LORD."

Because a "day of the Lord" was coming upon Peter's generation of Jews we read in Acts 2:40, "With many other words he [Peter] warned them; and he pleaded with them, 'Save yourselves from this corrupt generation.'"

If we view "the last days" as a metaphor for the entire New Covenant Age then we should be open to the possibility of our Bibles getting thicker because of new revelations from God. However, if "the last days" ended in A.D. 70 – then so did God's revelation for Scripture, which ensures that our Canon is complete. But if "the last days" truly refer to the entire New Covenant Age then our view of the future is summarized by II Timothy 3:1-5,

> "But mark this [Timothy]: There will be terrible times in the last days. ²People will be lovers of themselves, lovers of money, boastful, proud, abusive, disobedient to their parents, ungrateful, unholy, ³without love, unforgiving, slanderous, without self-control, brutal, not lovers of the good, ⁴treacherous, rash, conceited, lovers of pleasure rather than lovers of God – ⁵having a form of godliness but denying its power."

Is this really what God the Son came to earth to achieve? No. It is what He came to overcome. The Apostle Paul ends II Timothy 3:5 with this command to Timothy, "Have nothing to do with them." The people Paul described in verses 1-5 were alive when Paul and Timothy lived, which is why a "day of the Lord" was on the horizon. Any nation that is characterized by II Timothy 3:1-5 can expect a "day of the Lord" – unless there is repentance.

Scriptures referred to but not quoted:

John 12:19, "So the Pharisees said to one another, 'See, this is getting us nowhere. Look how the whole world ["kosmos" – referring to the land of Israel] has gone after him'" [speaking of Christ]!

Matthew 24:42-44, "Therefore keep watch, because you [the Christians of Christ's day] do not know on what day your Lord will come. [43]But understand this: If the owner of the house had known at what time of night the thief was coming, he would have kept watch and would not have let his house be broken into. [44]So you also must be ready, because the Son of Man will come at an hour when you do not expect him."

Galatians 4:9, "But now that you know God – or rather are known by God – how is it that you are turning back to those weak and miserable principles [stoixeia]? Do you wish to be enslaved by them all over again?"

Colossians 2:8 and 20, "See to it that no one takes you captive through hollow and deceptive philosophy, which depends on human tradition and the basic principles [stoixeia] of this world rather than on Christ. [20]Since you died with Christ to the basic principles [stoixeia] of this world, why, as though you still belonged to it, do you submit to its rules?"

Hebrews 5:12 [NASB], "For though by this time you ought to be teachers, you have need for some one to teach you the elementary principles [stoixeia] of the oracles of God, and you have come to need milk and not solid food."

I Samuel 3:1, "The boy Samuel ministered before the LORD under Eli. In those days the word of the LORD was rare; there were not many visions."

II Chronicles 32:32, "The other events of Hezekiah's reign and his acts of devotion are written in the vision of the prophet Isaiah …"

Daniel 7:1, "In the first year of Belshazzar king of Babyon, Daniel had a dream, and visions passed through his mind as he was lying on his bed. He wrote down the substance of his dream."

Amos 3:7, "Surely the Sovereign LORD does nothing without revealing his plan to his servants the prophets."

Daniel 9:24-27, "Seventy 'sevens' are decreed for your people [Old Covenant Israel] and your holy city to finish transgression, to put an end to sin [Old Covenant Israel was habitually unfaithful to God], to atone for wickedness, to bring in everlasting righteousness [this is speaking of the atoning work of Christ], to seal up [bring to an end] vision and prophecy [which would complete the Canon] and to anoint the most holy [God's new temple – the Church. Everything mentioned in Daniel 9:24 was accomplished during the last days of Old Covenant Israel]. [25]Know and understand this: From the issuing of the decree [of Cyrus recorded in Ezra 1:1-3, in fulfillment of Isaiah 44:28 – 45:4 and Jeremiah 29:10] to restore and rebuild Jerusalem until the Anointed One, the ruler [Cyrus was called God's "anointed" in Isaiah 45:1. And so it seems that another anointed one would be appointed by God to destroy the rebuilt Jerusalem and temple. This anointed one was also a ruler] … [26]The people of the ruler who will come will destroy the city and the sanctuary [which occurred in A.D. 70]. The end will come like a flood: War will continue until the end, and desolations have been decreed. [27]He [the ruler whose people will destroy Jerusalem and the temple] will confirm a covenant with many for one 'seven.' [Nero indeed made promises to the Romans when he came to the throne. Those promises were kept for the first part of his rule, which was known as the golden years. But then Nero became utterly corrupt and the Jews stopped making sacrifices for Rome and revolted in A.D. 66]. In the middle of the 'seven' he will put an end to sacrifice and offering. And on a wing of the temple he will set up an abomination that causes desolation [I believe Nero's abomination is what he did to God's new temple, the Church], until the end that is decreed is poured out on him.'" In Matthew 24:15, Jesus told His disciples that they would see this abomination spoken of by Daniel. And because Daniel 9:27 reveals that this ruler would be cut off, the Apostle Paul could confidently proclaim in II Thessalonians 2:3, that the man of lawlessness was doomed to destruction.

CHAPTER 8:

The New Heavens and New Earth Isaiah 65 and 66

One of the most thrilling passages in all the Bible is a vision the Apostle John was given when he was a prisoner on the island of Patmos [in modern day Greece] almost two thousand years ago. It is recorded in Revelation 21:1-4 and takes us as far into the future as God has sovereignly determined,

> "Then I saw a new heaven and a new earth, for the first heaven and the first earth had passed away, and there was no longer any sea. ²I saw the Holy City, the new Jerusalem, coming down out of heaven from God [the heavenly Jerusalem is also spoken of in Hebrews 12:22-23], prepared as a bride [referring to Christ's completed Church] beautifully dressed for her husband. ³And I heard a loud voice from the throne saying, 'Now the dwelling of God is with men, and he will live with them [upon the new earth, the ultimate temple of God]. They will be his people, and God himself will be with them and be their God. ⁴He will wipe every tear from their eyes. There will be no more death or mourning or crying or pain, for the old order of things has passed away'" [underlining is mine].

This text is describing the grand event of God's people receiving their final and ultimate bodies. In II Corinthians 5:1 the Apostle Paul refers to our present bodies, which are made from the dust of this earth, as tents. This indicates they are temporary dwelling places for our spirits, which separate from our bodies at the time of death and are taken by Jesus to the Father's house. The Apostle Paul likens our heavenly bodies to a building which is eternal in duration. However, just as our present bodies are well-suited for life on this present earth and our heavenly bodies are well-suited for life in heaven – the ultimate destination of God's people is the new earth described in Revelation 21:1-4. I believe the bodily resurrection of all God's people, from the days of Adam until the end of time, will take place when God ushers in the new heaven and new earth. Why will all of God's people get their resurrection bodies at the same time? Because those glorified bodies will be perfectly suited for life on the new earth. And it is very fitting that our heavenly bodies will be incorporated into our resurrection bodies because the new earth will be the ultimate temple of God and the place of His special presence forever.

What does John mean when he says that the new earth will have no sea? In a book such as Revelation, which is rich in Old Testament references and imagery, Isaiah 57:20 may provide the answer, "But the wicked are like the tossing sea, which cannot rest, whose waves cast up mire and mud." John may simply be telling us that there will be no wicked people on the new earth foretold in Revelation 21. The only people who will enjoy that ultimate phase of God's kingdom are the people of God in glorified bodies that never die and never again suffer sorrow or pain. The Apostle Paul expresses this same truth in I Corinthians 15:50-54,

> "I declare to you brothers, that flesh and blood cannot inherit the kingdom of God [in its ultimate form], nor does the perishable [people in flesh and blood bodies] inherit the imperishable. [51]Listen, I tell you a mystery: We [followers of Christ] will not all sleep [die], but we will all be changed – [52]in a flash, in the twinkling of an eye, at the last trumpet. For the trumpet will sound, the dead will be raised imperishable, and we [Christians who are physically alive at the time of that event] will be changed. [53]For the perishable must clothe itself with the imperishable, and the mortal with immortality ... [54]then the saying that is written [in Isaiah 25:8] will come true: 'Death has been swallowed up in victory.'"

However, the new heavens and new earth spoken of in Isaiah 65:17-25 and 66:22-24 are not referring to the Eternal State because both of these texts speak about death. How then are we to understand the Bible's use of new heaven and new earth? Let me explain by comparing it with a parallel idea. Our Lord Jesus came to earth over 2,000 years ago to begin His kingdom [Matthew 4:17], which has been steadily growing as more and more people embrace Christ as their Savior and Lord. Colossians 1:13-14 states,

> "For he has rescued us from the dominion of darkness and brought us into the kingdom of the Son he loves, [14]in whom we have redemption, the forgiveness of sins."

All genuine Christians are in Christ's kingdom. And yet the Apostle Paul declares in I Corinthians 15:50, "... flesh and blood cannot inherit the kingdom of God." What gives? Are we in the kingdom or not? Yes we are, but in I Corinthians 15:50 Paul is referring to the ultimate phase of the kingdom of God – which is the Eternal State. No one enters into that form of the kingdom with the flesh and blood bodies we have now. And so biblically speaking, there is a form of the kingdom in which we now live and a form of the kingdom which is yet future.

In the same way, there is a form of the new heavens and new earth that was ushered in by the New Covenant. All human beings who are regenerated through repentance and faith in Christ become a part of God's New Covenant people. Listen to the Apostle Paul as he describes followers of Christ in II Corinthians 5:17, "… if anyone is in Christ, he is a new creation; the old has gone, the new has come!" The new creation of regeneration starts in the unseen spiritual realm of the human will and then changes our values and actions. As a Christian I still have the same flesh and blood body I had before I was born again and became a part of Christ's new humanity. And even though the Apostle Paul could accurately refer to Christians in flesh and blood bodies as "new creations" – we will not be new creations in the fullest sense – until we gain our glorified bodies at the time Christ comes to raise the dead and usher in the Eternal State. The spiritual beginning of the new heaven and earth was at Pentecost. It was a small beginning. But as more and more people become "new creations" and Christ's kingdom continues to grow upon the earth, then the more this earth becomes "new". Nevertheless, this great work of God will not come to full fruition until the final advent of Christ, when He ushers in the Eternal State, which is the ultimate expression of the "new earth" described in Revelation 21:1-4.

To verify this let's take a closer look at Isaiah 65 which begins by foretelling: (1) God's call to the Gentiles after Christ's finished work at the cross – and (2) His severe judgment upon disobedient Old Covenant Israel. However, even during the last days of Old Covenant Israel [which ended in A.D. 70], there was a remnant of believing Jews who faithfully followed Christ and shared the good news of the gospel – starting at Jerusalem as foretold in Isaiah 65:17-18,

> "For behold, I create new heavens and a new earth, and the former things shall not be remembered or come into mind. [18]But be glad and rejoice forever in that which I create; for behold, I create Jerusalem to be a joy, and her people to be a gladness."

The New Covenant Church, which is the temple of God upon the earth today, was birthed at Jerusalem in Acts 2 and was initially composed of Jewish believers. However, from Jerusalem the gospel went out into all the world with the number of Gentile believers quickly surpassing the number of Jewish believers. Unfortunately, the majority of Jewish people in the days of the Apostles became hardened to the gospel. But that heartbreak will not go on indefinitely, as the Apostle Paul explains in Romans 11:25-31,

> "… Israel has experienced a hardening in part until the full number of the Gentiles has come in. And so all Israel will be saved [God's new Israel is composed of both believing Jews and Gentiles], as it is written: 'The deliverer will come from Zion [Jerusalem – in fulfillment of Isaiah 2:2-3]; he will turn godlessness away from Jacob [referring to the Jewish people]. [27]And this is my covenant with them when I take away their sins' [promised in Jeremiah 31:34]. [28]As far as the gospel is concerned, they are enemies on

your account [many unbelieving Jews in Paul's day had a very low opinion of Gentiles]; but as far as election is concerned, they are loved on account of the patriarchs, [29]for God's gifts and his call are irrevocable [Genesis 22:16-18]. [30]Just as you [Gentiles] who were at one time disobedient to God have now received mercy as a result of their [unbelieving Jews] disobedience, [31]so they too have now become disobedient in order that they too may now receive mercy as a result of God's mercy to you."

It seems that at some point in the future, God's blessings upon myriads and myriads of Gentile believers will make the unbelieving Jews jealous and the vast majority of them will turn to Christ. Isaiah 19:23-24 testifies that the day will come when,

"The Egyptians and Assyrians [present day Middle East] will worship together. [24]In that day Israel will be the third, along with Egypt and Assyria, a blessing on the earth."

There is a strong hint in those verses that the Gentile neighbors of Israel – who come to Christ in mass will lead to unbelieving Israel coming to Christ in mass. And when that happens Isaiah 65:19 will be fulfilled, "I will rejoice in Jerusalem and be glad in my people; no more shall be heard in it the sound of weeping and the cry of distress." Even when the Apostle Paul was alive he commanded both Jew and Gentile Christians to do the following,

"Rejoice in the Lord always; again I will say, Rejoice ... [6]do not be anxious about anything, but in everything by prayer and supplication with thanksgiving let your requests be made known to God. [7]And the peace of God, which surpasses all understanding, will guard your hearts and minds in Christ Jesus" [Philippians 4:4-7 ESV].

The more people who come to Christ, the more rejoicing and the less weeping there will be. But Isaiah is not yet finished describing God's future blessings destined to come upon people in flesh and blood bodies. Isaiah 65:20 boldly declares this promise,

> "No more shall there be in it [a believing Israel] an infant who lives but a few days, or an old man who does not live out his years; he who dies at a hundred will be thought a mere youth; he who fails to reach a hundred will be considered accursed."

Because our faith in God's promises tend to be the size of a mustard seed, God has already shown that He can accomplish the kind of blessings described in Isaiah 65:20. Way back in Genesis 5 God lists seven people, starting with Adam, who lived to be over nine-hundred years old. Do you think there was a lot of infant mortality at the time those people lived? The blessings of modern science, technology and medicine are the result of a biblical worldview. In the United States during the year of 1900, 1 out of 6 children died before their first birthday. In 2011 only 1 out of 150 children died before the age of 1. Life expectancy in the United States in 1900 was 47 years. In 2011 it was 78 years. Life expectancy world-wide in 1820 was 26 years. In 2011 it was 66 years.

Isaiah 65:21-23 continues to speak about future blessings upon the peoples of the earth during this New Covenant Age, which at this particular time in history is plagued by socialistic practices which do not respect private property,

"They shall build houses and inhabit them; they shall plant vineyards and eat their fruit. [22]They shall not build and another inhabit; they shall not plant and another eat; for like the days of a tree shall the days of my people be, and my chosen shall long enjoy the work of their hands. [23]They shall not labor in vain [due to civil government garnishing large portions of their earnings] or bear children for calamity, for they shall be the offspring of the blessed of the LORD, and their descendants with them."

These kind of promises also appear in Micah 4:4, "Every man will sit under his own vine and under his own fig tree, and no one will make them afraid, for the LORD Almighty has spoken" [underlining is mine]. The blessings of Micah 4:4 and Isaiah 65:21-23 imply a deep respect for private property, which is grounded upon the Eighth and Tenth Commandments. David Bahnsen states a well-known economic reality in his book, There's No Free Lunch,

"History leaves no doubt – where there is no private property, or legal system to defend such, chaos reigns. Where there is a healthy respect for the God-given concept of private property and private ownership, a flourishing civilization becomes possible."

Isaiah 65:24-25 declares,

"Before they call I will answer; while they are yet speaking I will hear. [25]The wolf and the lamb shall graze together; the lion shall eat straw like the ox and dust shall be the serpent's food. They shall not hurt or destroy in all my holy mountain."

Verse 25 is a profound picture of peace. Isaiah 35:9 speaks in a similar manner about the blessings of those who walk on the Way of

Holiness, "No lion shall be there, nor shall any ravenous beast come upon it; they shall not be found there, but the redeemed shall walk there." The absence of the lion and ravenous beast seems to refer to the absence of the wicked attacking the righteous. This is still a future reality.

There are some who contend that Isaiah 65:19-25 was Isaiah's best effort to communicate truths about the Eternal State. It is claimed that because people in Isaiah's day could not comprehend the concept of never dying – it caused Isaiah to speak about long life spans. This seems very weak in light of Isaiah 25:8, which refers to God swallowing up death forever. The Apostle Paul applies that verse to the Eternal State in I Corinthians 15:54.

Let's move on to Isaiah 66, since it also refers to a new heaven and new earth. But first we need to note an important truth tucked away in the first verse of Isaiah 66,

> "This is what the LORD says: 'Heaven is my throne, and the earth is my footstool [hadom]. Where is the house you will build for me? Where will my resting place be?"

God's footstool [hadom], appears five other times in the Old Testament and always refers to God's temple at Jerusalem. This is an important truth that relates to God's irrevocable promise to Abraham, Isaac and Jacob. Therefore, I will give a short explanation as to why that is true in the addendum to this chapter.

Let's return to Isaiah 66:2-3,

> "This is the one I esteem: he who is humble and contrite in spirit,

and trembles at my word [one who fears God]. ³But [in Isaiah's day] whoever sacrifices a bull is like one who kills a man, and whoever offers a lamb, like one who breaks a dog's neck; whoever makes a grain offering is like one who presents pig's blood, and whoever burns memorial incense, like one who worships an idol. They have chosen their own ways, and their souls delight in their abominations."

In verse 3, Isaiah is referring to unbelieving Jews in his day who merely went through the motions of serving God, but their hearts were far away – which made them a stench in God's nostrils. In Matthew 15:7-9 and John 8:42-47, Jesus characterized the unbelieving Jews of His day in that same way. Isaiah 66:4 reveals the consequences for doing so, "so I also will choose harsh treatment for them and will bring upon them what they dread ..." Isaiah lived to see the ten northern tribes of Israel defeated and carried off by the Assyrians in 722 B.C. About a hundred and thirty-five years later the southern tribes of Judah were defeated by the Babylonians and most of the survivors were carried out of the land. But the Jewish people who trembled at God's Word not only survived the attacks of the Assyrians and Babylonians, but continued to faithfully serve God in the countries to which they were taken. Many of their descendants enjoyed the privilege of being able to return to their homeland during the days of Daniel, Haggai, Zechariah, Ezra and Nehemiah. At the time of Ezra and Nehemiah there was a significant revival which led to a season of great expansion and blessings for Israel. In the same way most Jewish followers of Christ survived the fall of Jerusalem at the hands of the Romans. Isaiah 66:7-12 aptly foretells how God would use Jewish followers of Christ to give birth to the New Covenant Church, which I Peter 2:9 refers to as a holy nation:

> "Before she goes into labor, she gives birth; before the pains come upon her, she delivers a son. [8]Who has ever heard of such a thing? Who has ever seen such things? Can a country be born in a day or a nation be brought forth in a moment? Yet no sooner is Zion in labor than she gives birth to her children [the New Covenant Church was birthed at Jerusalem on the Day of Pentecost and has been continually growing ever since] … [10]'Rejoice with Jerusalem and be glad for her, all you who love her; rejoice greatly with her … [11]For you [Gentile followers of Christ] will nurse and be satisfied at her comforting breasts; you will drink deeply and delight in her overflowing abundance.' [12]For this is what the LORD says: 'I will extend peace to her like a river, and the wealth of nations like a flooding stream … ' "

In order for righteousness and blessings to continue moving forward, God must judge the unrepentant wicked who oppose the righteous – as revealed in Isaiah 66:15-19,

> "See, the LORD is coming with fire, and his chariots are like a whirlwind; he will bring down his anger with fury, and his rebuke with flames of fire. [16]For with fire and with his sword the LORD will execute judgment upon all men [referring to the Middle East, which was the biblical world of the Old Testament] … [19]I will set a sign among them [the believing Jews of Isaiah and Jeremiah's day], and I will send some of those who survive to the nations … and to the distant islands that have not heard of my fame or seen my glory. They will proclaim my glory among the nations."

This was true of faithful dispersed Jews who were carried out of their land by the Assyrians and Babylonians; and also true of the Jewish followers of Christ who survived the fall of Jerusalem and went on to share the good news of the gospel all over the world – along with Gentile followers of Christ. What will the gospel achieve among the nations? Isaiah 66:20-21 states the following promise,

> "And they will bring all your brothers, from all the nations, to my holy mountain in Jerusalem as an offering to the LORD – on horses, in chariots and wagons, and on mules and camels," says the LORD. "They will bring them, as the Israelites bring their grain offerings, to the temple of the LORD in ceremonially clean vessels. [21]And I will select some of them also to be priests and Levites,' says the LORD."

This was fulfilled during the time of Ezra and Nehemiah, but in a greater sense during this New Covenant Age. When I was in Jerusalem during the 1990's with a group of about fifty pastors, who function as New Covenant priests and Levites, we witnessed busloads of Christians from all over the world pulling into Jerusalem to see where their Savior and Lord paid the penalty of their sins in full.

Isaiah 66:22-24 goes on to speak about more great blessings to come,

> "As the new heavens and the new earth that I make will endure before me,' declares the LORD, 'so will your name and descendants endure. [23]From one New Moon to another and from one Sabbath to another, all mankind will come and bow down before me,' says the LORD" [According to Jeremiah Johnston in his 2019 book Unimaginable: What Our World Would Be Like Without Christianity, there are presently 70,000 people a day coming to Christ]. [24]'And they will go out and look upon

the dead bodies of those who rebelled against me; their worm will not die, nor will their fire be quenched, and they will be loathsome to all mankind.'"

Verse 24 could be an indication that a famous quote by the German philosopher Hegel may one day be proven false, "History teaches us that man learns nothing from history." As the Church grows and matures, the Lord will help us and those we influence to remember and learn from what God has done to wicked people in the past. The New Testament often quotes from Psalm 2 and Psalm 110, which speak about the ascended Lord Jesus. Both of these Psalms warn about severe judgments upon the wicked carried out by Christ from His throne in heaven [see Psalm 2:8-12 and Psalm 110:5-6]. Currently many Christians believe the world is worse today than ever before. That is a stunning lack of historic knowledge which goes along with Jorge Manrique's insightful comment, "Any time gone by was better." Much more awareness of history and what God is currently doing worldwide needs to take place. From Jerusalem to Timbuktu, by Brian C. Stiller, is a helpful book for revealing what God is doing worldwide.

Addendum: Footstool (hadom)

Psalm 110, written by David, is one of the most quoted psalms in the New Testament, "The LORD [God the Father] says to my Lord [God the Son]: 'Sit at my right hand until I make your enemies a footstool for your feet.'" One of the insights of Psalm 110 is that it records a world-changing transaction between God the Father and

God the Son. This transaction was planned before the creation of the world [Ephesians 1:4], but not officially entered into until the time of Christ's ascension. Hebrews 10:12-13 states,

> "But when this priest [Christ] had offered for all time one sacrifice for sins, he sat down at the right hand of God. Since that time he waits for his enemies to be made his footstool."

There are two critical questions which arise from Psalm 110 – (1) Who are Christ's enemies and (2) what does God mean when He promises to make Christ's enemies into a footstool for His feet? The answer to the first question is that ALL people who knowingly practice sin and refuse to repent are living at enmity with Christ. The Apostle Paul teaches this truth in Colossians 1:21-22,

> "Once you were alienated from God and were enemies in your minds because of your evil behavior. But now he has reconciled you by Christ's physical body through death to present you holy in his sight, without blemish and free from accusation."

Romans 5:10 states,

> "For if while we were enemies we were reconciled to God by the death of his Son, much more, now that we are reconciled shall we be saved by his life."

This leads us to our second question: What is the meaning of "footstool"? Normally this word is viewed by scholars as a symbol for defeated and crushed enemies. Archeology has shown that in Old Testament times kings would have the names or images of conquered enemies engraved on their footstools. And indeed Psalm 110:5-6 speaks of Christ's enemies being crushed beneath His feet. Jesus also supports this meaning for footstool in Mark 12:36. However, verses

2-3 of Psalm 110 tell us,

"The LORD [God the Father] will extend your [God the Son's] mighty scepter from Zion; you will rule in the midst of your enemies. Your troops will be willing on your day of battle."

Where does Christ find willing troops to serve him since unsaved people are at enmity against Him? Christ's willing troops were once enemies who have been saved by God's grace. When lost people are saved they become temples of God and willing troops for King Jesus. The Apostle Paul writes to the believers at Corinth, "Don't you know that you yourselves are God's temple and that God's Spirit lives in you?" [I Corinthians 3:16]

There is a saying which goes as follows, "The New Testament is in the Old Testament – concealed; and the Old Testament is in the New Testament – revealed." In the Old Testament God's stone temple at Jerusalem was called his footstool, as we see in the following verses:

I Chronicles 28:2, "King David rose to his feet and said: 'Listen to me, my brothers and my people. I had it in my heart to build a house as a place of rest for the ark of the covenant of the LORD, **for the footstool [temple] of our God**, and I made plans to build it'" [emphasis is mine].

Psalm 99:5, "Exalt the LORD our God and worship at his footstool; he is holy."

Psalm 132:7-8, "Let us go to his dwelling place; let us worship at his footstool - arise, O LORD, and come to your resting place, you and the ark of your might."

Lamentations 2:1 [written after Jerusalem and the temple were destroyed by the Babylonians], "How the Lord has covered the

Daughter of Zion with the cloud of his anger! He has hurled down the splendor of Israel from heaven to earth; he has not remembered his footstool in the day of anger."

There is only one other reference to footstool (hadom) in the Old Testament – Isaiah 66:1, "The earth is the LORD's footstool …" It would seem that the earth was initially created by God to be a place of His special presence – His temple. Mankind's fall into sin has changed that initial reality, but only temporarily. The new earth of Revelation 21 will fully be God's temple. Does the New Testament ever use the word "footstool" as a synonym for temple or holy place? Yes, in Hebrews 10:11-14 we read:

> "Day after day every [Levitical] priest stands and performs his religious duties; again and again he offers the same sacrifices, which can never take away sins [the Old Covenant temple, where Levitical priests offered animal sacrifices, was a temporary provision for sin. However, by the time Hebrews was written it had been made obsolete by Christ's death on the cross]. But when this priest [Christ, a priest after the order of Melchizedek] had offered for all time one sacrifice for sins, he sat down at the right hand of God. Since that time he waits for his enemies to be made his **footstool**, <u>because by one sacrifice he has made perfect forever those who are being made holy</u>" [bold print and underlining are mine].

There are times when God makes Christ's enemies into footstools by crushing them. The first example of this was the fall of Jerusalem in A.D. 70 [Luke 21:20-22]. Nevertheless, God's preferred way of dealing with Christ's enemies is to redeem them and make them into temples [footstools]. John 3:17, "For God did not send his Son into the world to condemn the world, but to save the world through him." For over 1900 years God has been making Christ's enemies into footstools – if we have eyes to see. And one day when Christ returns to raise the dead and usher in the Eternal State, this earth will fully become God's temple.

Scriptures referred to but not quoted:

Hebrews 12:22-23, "But you have come to Mount Zion, to the heavenly Jerusalem, the city of the living God. You have come to thousands upon thousands of angels in joyful assembly, [23]to the church of the firstborn, whose names are written in heaven ..."

Matthew 4:17, "From that time on Jesus began to preach, 'Repent, for the kingdom of heaven is near.'"

Isaiah 2:2-3, "In the last days [of the Old Covenant Age in which Isaiah lived] the mountain of the LORD'S temple [Christ's New Covenant Church] will be established as chief among the mountains; it will be raised above the hills, and all nations will stream to it. [3]Many peoples will come and say, 'Come, let us go up to the mountain of the LORD, to the house of the God of Jacob. He will teach us his ways, so that we may walk in his paths.' The law will go out from Zion, the word of the LORD from Jerusalem" [commanded by the resurrected Christ in Acts 1:3-8 and acted upon in Acts chapters 2 through 28].

Jeremiah 31:34, "No longer will a man teach his neighbor, or a man his brother, saying, 'Know the LORD,' because they will all know me, from the least of them to the greatest," declares the LORD. "For I will forgive their wickedness and will remember their sins no more."

Matthew 15:7-9, "You hypocrites! Isaiah was right when he prophesied about you: ⁸'These people honor me with their lips, but their hearts are far from me. ⁹They worship me in vain; their teachings are but rules taught by men.'"

John 8:42-47, "Jesus said to them, 'If God were your Father, you would love me, for I came from God and now am here ... ⁴³Why is my language not clear to you? Because you are unable to hear what I say. ⁴⁴You belong to your father, the devil ... ⁴⁷He who belongs to God hears what God says. The reason you do not hear is that you do not belong to God.'"

I Peter 2:9, "But you are a chosen people, a royal priesthood, <u>a holy nation</u>, a people belonging to God, that you may declare the praises of him who called you out of darkness into his wonderful light" [underlining is mine].

Psalm 2:8-12, "Ask of me, and I will make the nations your inheritance, the ends of the earth your possession. ⁹You will rule them with an iron scepter; you will dash them to pieces like pottery. ¹⁰Therefore, you kings, be wise; be warned, you rulers of the earth. ¹¹Serve the LORD with fear and rejoice with trembling. ¹²Kiss the Son, lest he be angry and you be destroyed in your way, for his wrath can flare up in a moment. Blessed are all who take refuge in him."

Psalm 110:1-6, "The LORD [God the Father] says to my Lord [God the Son]: 'Sit at my right hand until I make your enemies a footstool for your feet.' ²The LORD will extend your mighty scepter from Zion; you will rule in the midst of your enemies ... ⁵The Lord [referring to the ascended Lord Jesus] is at your right hand [referring to God the Father]; he [the ascended Lord Jesus] will crush kings on the day of his wrath. ⁶He will judge the nations, heaping up the dead and crushing the rulers of the whole earth."

Ephesians 1:4, "For he chose us in him before the creation of the world to be holy and blameless in his sight."

Mark 12:36, "David himself, speaking by the Holy Spirit, declared: 'The Lord said to my Lord: "Sit at my right hand until I put your enemies under your feet.""'"

Luke 21:20-22, "When you see Jerusalem being surrounded by armies, you will know that its desolation is near. [21]Then let those who are in Judea flee to the mountains, let those in the city get out, and let those in the country not enter the city. [22]For this is the time of punishment in fulfillment of all that has been written."

CHAPTER 9:
Support for the Partial Preterist Viewpoint of Revelation

The word "preterist" is taken from a Latin word meaning "past". When we apply it to the book of Revelation it means that the judgments spoken of in chapters 1-19, refer to events that were in the near future when the Apostle John wrote it, but from our 21ˢᵗ century perspective these judgments have already taken place. Full preterism believes all of the book of Revelation is speaking about past events. Partial preterism believes that chapters 20 – 22 contain important ramifications concerning Christ's crucifixion and additional truths that take us all the way to the end of the New Covenant Age and beginning of the Eternal State. However, both the first and last chapters of Revelation give evidence that the near at hand judgments John describes would be carried out in his day. Revelation 1:1 states, "The revelation of Jesus Christ, which God gave him to show his servants what must soon take place." Two verses later John is again told that "the time is near" [engus]. In Revelation 22:10, an angel tells John, "Do not seal up the words of the prophecy of this book, because the time is near" [engus].

In light of the meaning of "near" [engus] all through the New Testament, the natural understanding is that the terrible judgments described in this book were close at hand when John was writing. This is particularly apparent when Revelation 22:10, is compared with Daniel 8:26, where an angel tells Daniel, "The vision of the evenings and mornings that has been given you is true, but seal up the vision, for it concerns the distant future." The events spoken of in Daniel 8:1-25, extended from the fall of Babylon [538 B.C.] to the death of Antiochus Epiphanes [in 164 B.C. – which was 386 years later]. Notice that Daniel was instructed to seal up the scroll because the events of that chapter were in the distant future. In contrast, an angel tells the Apostle John at the end of his vision in Revelation 22:6 and 10,

> "These words are trustworthy and true. The Lord, the God of the spirits of the prophets, sent his angel to show his servants the things which must soon take place … [10]Then he told me, 'Do not seal up the words of the prophecy of this book, because the time is near.'"

How can the judgments of Revelation be called "near" in John's day, if they have not yet been fulfilled almost two thousand years later? Let's now read Revelation 1:7 in a more literal manner,

> "Look, he [Christ] is coming with the clouds, and every eye will see him, even those who pierced him; and all the tribes of the land will mourn because of him."

Who are the tribes of the land spoken of all through the Old Testament? The twelve tribes of Israel. Who are those who pierced Christ? The New Testament teaches that it was the generation of Jews who falsely condemned Christ, had him crucified at the hands of the Romans and then went on to persecute His followers. Notice the following passages which testify to this truth:

> Acts 2:23-26, "This man [Jesus] was handed over to you [the unbelieving Jews of Peter's day] by God's set purpose and foreknowledge; and you, with the help of wicked men [the Romans], put him to death by nailing him to the cross … [26]Therefore let all Israel be assured of this: God has made this Jesus, whom you crucified, both Lord and Christ."

> Acts 3:13-15, "The God of Abraham, Isaac and Jacob, the God of our fathers, has glorified his servant Jesus. You [unbelieving Jews] handed him over to be killed, and you disowned him before Pilate … [15]You killed the author of life, but God raised him from the dead."

> I Thessalonians 2:14-16, "… God's churches in Judea … suffered from the Jews, [15]who killed the Lord Jesus and the prophets and also drove us out. They displease God and are hostile to all men [16]in their effort to keep us from speaking to the Gentiles so that they may be saved. In this way they always heap up their sins to the limit. The wrath of God has come upon them at last" [their doom was certain].

> Matthew 27:24-25, "When Pilate saw that he was getting nowhere … he took water and washed his hands in front of the crowd. 'I am innocent of this man's blood,' he said. 'It is your responsibility.' [25]All the people answered, 'Let his blood be on us and on our children!'"

That generation of Jews accepted full responsibility for Christ's death and had the guilt of all the blood of God's prophets laid upon them by Jesus Himself [Matthew 23:33-36]. What does Revelation 1:7 mean by Christ coming in the clouds? It meant that the ascended Lord Jesus was going to judge those who pierced Him and persecuted His followers. This did not require a bodily coming of Christ to achieve. The ascended Lord Jesus can judge nations the same way God the Father judged nations in Old Testament times. A close parallel to Revelation 1:7 is found in Matthew 24:30-34, again in a more literal translation,

> "At that time [after wars, famine, earthquakes, and a great falling away from the faith] the sign that the Son of Man is in heaven [in the seat of power] will appear, and all the tribes of the land will mourn. They will see the Son of Man coming on the clouds of the sky, with power and great glory … [33]Even so, when you [the disciples to whom Jesus was speaking] see all these things, you know that it is near ["engus" – referring to the fall of Jerusalem and the temple's destruction], right at the door. [34]I tell you the truth, this generation will certainly not pass away until all these things have happened."

The context of Matthew 24 is the destruction of Jerusalem – not the end of the world. John begins the book of Revelation by explaining that the time was near [engus] for the temple at Jerusalem to be destroyed, which was the official end of Old Covenant Israel. The book of Hebrews was written in the mid 60's and according to Hebrews 8:13 the Old Covenant Age with its animal sacrifices at the stone temple was just about to disappear.

Another indication that the Apostle John's vision pertained to soon coming events is that the seven churches of Revelation 2-3, were actual congregations which existed in John's day. The truths of Revelation were pertinent and instructive to those seven churches and all the other churches at that time in history. Indeed, there are truths and applications of what John wrote to these seven churches that are for all believers of every culture and generation that have followed. But if the original audience and context are overlooked, serious misunderstandings will result! Christ's words to the church at Philadelphia in Revelation 3:10-11 illustrate this truth,

> "Since you have kept my command to endure patiently, I will also keep you from the hour of trial that is going to come upon the whole world to test those who live on the earth. ¹¹I am coming soon."

Is this hour of trial referring to a seven year tribulation period at the end of our New Covenant Age? And is Jesus' statement, "I am coming soon," speaking about His Second Coming? Most certainly not. Who was Christ speaking to in this passage? He was speaking to the believers at Philadelphia who lived about two-thousand years ago. What did Christ promise them? That He would keep them from the hour of trial that was coming upon the whole world [oikoumena]. Was there an intense period of judgment that came upon the whole world over 1900 years ago? Yes, but the meaning of the Greek word translated – "whole world" [oikoumena]" is used in Luke 2:1 and is referring to the Roman Empire. Acts 11:28 also speaks about a famine spreading over all the world [oikoumena – Roman Empire] during the reign of Claudius [41-54 A.D.].

Revelation 3:10b uses two words that have a breadth of meaning,

> "… the hour of trial that is going to come upon the whole world [oikoumena – in this context it refers to the Roman Empire] to test those who live on the earth" [ghays].

The Greek word "ghays" often translated earth, can also be speaking about the land of a particular country. This word appears one-hundred and nine times in Matthew through I John – and most often refers to the whole earth. But it appears seventy-nine times in the book of Revelation – and most often refers to the land of Israel, which was the focus of Christ's judgment warnings in Luke 21:20-24,

> "When you see Jerusalem being surrounded by armies, you will know that its desolation is near. Then let those who are in Judea flee to the mountains … ²³There will be great distress in the land [ghays] and wrath against this people [Old Covenant Israel]. ²⁴They will fall by the sword and will be taken as prisoners to all the nations …"

Was there an hour of testing that came upon the Roman Empire and particularly the land of Israel shortly after John received this message? It all depends upon when the book of Revelation was written. If it was written around A.D. 65-68, then the answer is yes. In A.D. 68, Caesar Nero, the emperor of the Roman Empire, committed suicide leaving no heir to his throne. Many thought this was the end of the Roman Empire because all the Julio-Claudian emperors had been considered gods [there were temples, altars and priests dedicated to the worship of the Caesars all over the Roman Empire]. A question being asked at the time of Nero's death was: Could a non-god rule Rome? In a period of eighteen months the Roman Empire had four different emperors. Civil war raged in the streets of Rome. Finally, Vespasian [the general whom Nero ordered to crush the Jewish revolt] gained and kept the throne in

A.D. 69. Once he established control of the Roman Empire he sent his son Titus to conquer Jerusalem, which resulted in the city's total destruction – including the temple.

If the book of Revelation was written in A.D. 91-96 [as most commentaries say], would there have been powerful synagogues of Jews in Smyrna [Revelation 2:9] and Philadelphia [Revelation 3:9] – a mere twenty years after the nation of Israel was completely crushed? We must remember that in the period of A.D. 66-70 [from the time the Jews revolted against Rome – until Jerusalem fell], hundreds of thousands of Jews were killed and thousands more were carried off into slavery [just as Jesus foretold in Luke 21:24]. In A.D. 91-96, the Jews were a broken people who had no temple, no priesthood, no sacrifices. Revelation 3:7-13 makes much more sense if John wrote it before the Jews revolted in A.D. 66.

In Revelation 3:11 Jesus promised the believers at Philadelphia that He was coming soon [taxu]. Christ already warned the congregation at Ephesus that if they did not repent He would come and remove their candlestick [Revelation 2:5]. In Revelation 2:16 Christ warned the church at Pergamum that if they did not repent He would come soon [taxu] and deal with the false teachers in that congregation. He gave the same warning to the false teachers at Thyatira [Revelation 2:25]. He warned the church at Sardis that if they did not wake up He would come like a thief against them. Was Jesus speaking about His bodily return at the end of our age? Of course not. If the ascended Lord Jesus could come against churches in John's day could He not also come against the Roman Empire and unbelieving Israel without having to return in bodily form?

Revelation 13 and 17 are important chapters which provide key signposts to help us properly understand this book. In chapter 17:3-5 John is shown a vision of a woman with Babylon the Great, the Mother of Prostitutes and of the Abominations of the Earth, written on her forehead. This woman was riding on a scarlet beast with seven heads. Revelation 17:18 tells the identity of the woman – she is the great city. Revelation 11:8 identifies "the great city" as the place where the "Lord was crucified." This is referring to Jerusalem, which at the time Revelation was written represented apostate Old Covenant Israel. Unbelieving Israel was referred to as a harlot all through the Old Testament [see Isaiah 1:21; Jeremiah 3:1-2; Ezekiel 16:15-16]. But her greatest act of harlotry was in rejecting her Messiah.

What is the beast upon which the woman rides? Verses 9-10 of Revelation 17 explain that the seven heads of the beast represent seven hills. In the days of the New Testament Rome was well known as the "city of seven hills" [it was stamped on Roman coins]. Verse 10 informs us that the seven heads also represent seven kings [obviously Roman kings]. At the time John was writing the book of Revelation five of those kings had fallen [died], one was presently ruling, and one was yet to come – but would rule only for a short period of time. Who would be the first king of the Roman Empire as it existed in John's day? The ancient Roman historians Suetonius and Dio Cassius considered Julius Caesar to be the first king or emperor of the Roman

Empire as it existed in New Testament times. It was Julius Caesar who appointed Herod the Great to be king over the Jews. Herod referred to Julius Caesar as his king. The emperors who followed Julius Caesar all bore his name. If we start with Julius Caesar then the five kings who had fallen in Revelation 17:10 would be:

1. Julius Caesar (49-44 B.C.) He is the head that suffered a fatal wound that was miraculously healed according to Revelation 13:3. When Julius Caesar was assassinated it looked as if his line of rulership had ended. But this proved to be false because he had adopted his great-nephew, who against all odds became the next ruler over the Roman Empire – even though it took seventeen years to accomplish.

2. Caesar Augustus (27 B.C.-14 A.D.) He rose to that position because Julius Caesar had adopted him as his son, which gave him Caesar's name and his wealth. He was the emperor when Christ was born.

3. Caesar Tiberius (14-37 A.D.) He was the emperor when Christ was crucified.

4. Caesar Caligula (37-41 A.D.) He wanted to set up an image of himself in the Jewish temple.

5. Caesar Claudius (41-54 A.D.) He temporarily kicked all the Jews out of the city of Rome.

6. Caesar Nero (54-68 A.D.) He would be the reigning emperor

when John wrote Revelation and was the last of the Julio-Claudian line. He was a serious persecutor of the Church.

7. Galba (68-69 A.D.) He fought his way to the throne after Nero committed suicide, but only lasted seven months before being killed.

Strong support for Nero being the ruling king when John was receiving his visions is given in Revelation 13:18, "This calls for wisdom. If anyone has insight, let him calculate the number of the beast [Rome], for it is a man's number. His number is 666." The man John was identifying as 666 would be a person his original audience [the seven churches of Asia Minor] could identify and was closely associated with the Roman Empire. Nero qualifies on both counts. In ancient Hebrew each letter of the alphabet had a numerical value [as did Greek and Latin]. The name Caesar Nero in Hebrew equals 616. In Greek, which was the universal language of that time, the name Nero equals 955. But his Greek name was always pronounced Neron. Adding the Greek letter Nu [n] adds 50 to Nero's name, which then equals 1005. The Roman historian Suetonius tells of a puzzle game that was circulating around the Roman Empire in Nero's day. The game went as follows:

"Count the numerical values

Of the letters in Nero's name,

And in 'murdered his own mother':

You will find that their sum is the same."

"Murdered [killed] his own mother" in Greek equals 1005. Nero not only killed his mother but two of his wives as well. Because the seven churches John was writing to all shared the Greek language in common, John used the name Neron when he translated it into Hebrew. The Hebrew letter that replaces the Nu of Greek is Nun, which also equals 50 [look at Greek and Hebrew Lexicons to verify this]. Neron Caesar in Hebrew equals 666. Is it just a coincidence that Nero was the sixth and last of the Julio-Claudian Emperors and that the Hellenistic version of his name in Hebrew equals 666? If Nero was the reigning emperor when John wrote Revelation, then the book was written no later than A.D. 68 – because that is when Nero killed himself. I believe it was written in A.D. 65, just before unbelieving Israel revolted against the Roman Empire and was crushed for doing so. Why would the Apostle John speak of the woman [unbelieving Israel] as riding on the beast [Rome]? Because unbelieving Israel used Rome to do the dirty work of crucifying Christ! Acts 12:1-3 also informs us that king Herod was influenced by the Jews in his persecution of Christians.

Revelation 18:20 states that "the great city" [apostate Jerusalem] was being judged for the way she treated the saints, apostles and prophets. Verse 24 of the same chapter adds, "In her was found the blood of prophets and of the saints, and of all who have been killed on the earth." Let's compare these verses with the words of Jesus recorded in Luke 11:47-51,

"Woe to you [the generation of unbelieving Jews living when Christ spoke these words], because you build tombs for the prophets, and it was your forefathers who killed them. [48]So you testify that you approve of what your forefathers did; they killed the prophets, and you build their tombs. [49]Because of this, God in his wisdom said, 'I will send them prophets and apostles, some of whom they will kill and others they will persecute.' [50]Therefore this generation will be held responsible for the blood of all the prophets that has been shed since the beginning of the world... [51]Yes, I tell you, this generation will be held responsible for it all."

These verses strongly favor the partial preterist viewpoint, which maintains that the judgments spoken of in the book of Revelation came upon the generation of Jews who rejected Christ, persecuted His prophets [the Apostle Paul in particular] and had the guilt of all the righteous martyrs laid on them by Christ.

Revelation 18:2 states, "Fallen! Fallen is Babylon the Great! She has become a home for demons and a haunt for every evil spirit." Our Lord Jesus warned that this would happen to the generation of Jews who rejected and crucified Him. After characterizing that generation as "wicked and adulterous" – Christ then states in Matthew 12:43-45,

"When an evil spirit comes out of a man [Christ had cast out many demons from the unbelieving Jews], it goes through arid places seeking rest and does not find it. [44]Then it says, 'I will return to the house I left.' When it arrives, it finds the house unoccupied, swept clean and put in order [because the Jews as a nation rejected Christ, they were an unoccupied house]. [45]Then it goes and takes with it seven other spirits [the number of completion] more wicked than itself, and they go in and live there. And the final condition of that man is worse than the first. That is how it will be with this wicked generation."

When we take all these inspired evidences together, an overwhelming case emerges for: (1) an early date for the book of Revelation; and (2) that this book is speaking about the great judgment carried out by the ascended Christ upon the nation of Israel in John's day. It was a judgment that affected the entire Roman Empire and had a cleansing effect upon the Church. There is application for nations and believers today, but the original context is apostate Israel's judgment in A.D. 70.

We should also remember that Old Covenant Israel was doomed before the Jews ever entered the promise land. Listen to Deuteronomy 31:16-19,

> "And the LORD said to Moses: "You are going to rest with your fathers, and these people will soon prostitute themselves to the foreign gods of the land they are entering [which they did and continued to do throughout much of the Old Testament age]. They will forsake me and break the covenant I made with them. ¹⁷On that day I will become angry with them and forsake them; I will hide my face from them, and they will be destroyed. Many disasters and difficulties will come upon them, and on that day they will ask, 'Have not these disasters come upon us because our God is not with us?' ¹⁸And I will certainly hide my face on that day because of all their wickedness in turning to other gods. ¹⁹Now write down for yourselves this song and teach it to the Israelites and have them sing it, so that it may be a witness for me against them."

The last time we hear about the "Song of Moses" is in Revelation 15:3, which was sung during the seven last plagues poured out upon the great prostitute [unbelieving Israel – Revelation 17:1-2]. This was the death-knell for Old Covenant Israel. It is not speaking about doom for God's New Covenant people! The New Covenant is destined for success not failure. We do not see defeat when God speaks about His blessings under the New Covenant [Jeremiah 31:31-34].

Listen also to the Apostle Paul's great excitement about the blessings of the New Covenant recorded in II Corinthians 3:3-10,

> "You show that you [New Covenant believers] are a letter from Christ, the result of our ministry, written not with ink but with the Spirit of the living God, not on tablets of stone but on tablets of human hearts. ⁴Such confidence as this is ours through Christ before God. ⁵Not that we are competent in ourselves to claim anything for ourselves, but our competence comes from God. ⁶He has made us competent as ministers of a new covenant – not of the letter but of the Spirit; for the letter kills, but the Spirit gives life. ⁷Now if the ministry that brought death, which was engraved in letters on stone, came with glory [and it did] … ⁸will not the ministry of the Spirit be even more glorious? ⁹If the ministry that condemns men is glorious, how much more glorious is the ministry that brings righteousness! ¹⁰For what was glorious has no glory now in comparison with the surpassing glory."

God's moral law, written by the finger of God upon stone tablets, is the standard of right and wrong – which makes it extremely valuable. The problem is that the law reveals our sin but does not give us the power to overcome our sin. We can state this another way. The law tells us to fly from what is wrong and do what is right, but it gives us no wings for doing so. The good news of the gospel, when embraced in a saving way, causes us to enter into the New Covenant whereupon God's law is written anew on our minds and hearts [Hebrews 8:10]. This gives us the desire to obey God's law, but additionally the indwelling Holy Spirit gives us the power to obey it as we learn to yield to His ways. Therefore, when we enter into the New Covenant we are not only told to fly – we are given wings to do so.

When we believe God's promises it greatly pleases and glorifies God. It is the blessings of the New Covenant that will unlock the promises of God spoken of in the Old Testament. As followers of Christ we become the descendants of Abraham who will bless all the nations. We do not glorify God by ignoring His promises and declaring that everything is going to get worse during this long-awaited New Covenant Age. The Bible texts that are used to support that kind of pessimism have been wrongly interpreted – as I have endeavored to show in this book.

Scriptures referred to but not quoted:

Matthew 23:33-36, "You snakes! You brood of vipers! How will you escape being condemned to hell? ³⁴Therefore I am sending you prophets and wise men and teachers. Some of them you will kill and crucify; others you will flog in your synagogues and pursue from town to town. ³⁵And so upon you will come all the righteous blood that has been shed on earth, from the blood of righteous Abel to the blood of Zechariah son of Berekiah, whom you murdered between the temple and the altar. ³⁶I tell you the truth, all this will come upon this generation."

Revelation 2:9, "I know your afflictions and your poverty – yet you are rich! I know the slander of those who say they are Jews and are not, but are a synagogue of Satan."

Revelation 3:9, "I will make those who are of the synagogue of Satan, who claim to be Jews though they are not, but are liars – I will make them come and fall down at your feet and acknowledge that I have loved you."

Isaiah 1:21, "See how the faithful city [Jerusalem] has become a harlot!"

Jeremiah 3:1-2, "… But you [Israel] have lived as a prostitute with many lovers – would you now return to me?" declares the LORD. ²Look up to the barren heights and see. Is there any place where you have not been ravished? By the roadside you sat waiting for lovers, sat like a nomad in the desert. You have defiled the land with your prostitution and wickedness."

Ezekiel 16:15-16, "But you [Israel] trusted in your beauty and used your fame to become a prostitute. You lavished your favors on anyone who passed by and your beauty became his. ¹⁶You took some of your garments to make gaudy high places, where you carried on your prostitution."

Revelation 13:3, "One of the heads [which represented Roman Emperors] of the beast [the Roman Empire] seemed to have had a fatal wound, but the fatal wound had been healed. The whole world was astonished and followed the beast."

Acts 12:1-3, "It was about this time that King Herod arrested some who belonged to the church, intending to persecute them. [2]He had James, the brother of John, put to death with the sword. [3]When he saw that this pleased the Jews, he proceeded to seize Peter also."

Revelation 17:1-2, "One of the seven angels who had the seven bowls came and said to me, 'Come, I will show you the punishment of the great prostitute, who sits on many waters [Jerusalem had the allegiance of Jewish people from all over the Roman Empire]. [2]With her the kings of the earth committed adultery and the inhabitants of the earth were intoxicated with the wine of her adulteries."

Hebrews 8:10, "This is the covenant I will make with the house of Israel after that time," declares the LORD. "I will put my law in their minds and write it on their hearts. I will be their God, and they will be my people."

CHAPTER 10:
Revelation 20

Revelation 20 is the golden text of the now popular Premillennial viewpoint, as well as being a key chapter for both of the other millennial views [Amillennial and Postmillennial]. Therefore we need to look at it closely. Let's first summarize what the Premillennial view teaches: (1) There will be a future thousand-year age after Christ bodily returns to the earth. (2) The glorified Christ will rule over all the nations from His capital city in Jerusalem. (3) This thousand-year rule will begin wonderfully with only believers on the earth, but it will end in a sizeable rebellion against the glorified Christ and His followers.

The Premillennial viewpoint was not popular among orthodox, evangelical Christians for about fifteen hundred years after Augustine rejected it sometime around A.D. 400. I should also point out that Revelation 20 is the only text in the Bible where a grammatical case can be made for a thousand-year rule of Christ on earth after He comes to raise the dead. To have only one text that explicitly backs up a viewpoint, and to have that text contained in the most difficult book of the Bible – is to stand on shaky ground. The interpretation of Revelation 20, used by Premillennialists, is grammatically permissible but not grammatically necessary; and more importantly it leads to theological contradiction as I will attempt to point out in this chapter. Let's now read Revelation 20:1-3,

> "And I saw an angel coming down out of heaven, having the key to the Abyss [domain of darkness] and holding in his hand a great chain. ²He seized the dragon, that ancient serpent, who is the devil, or Satan, and bound him for a thousand years. ³He cast him into the Abyss, and locked and sealed it over him, to keep him from deceiving the nations [Gentiles] anymore until the thousand years were ended. After that, he must be released for a little while."

Question: According to the Premillennial view who are the nations of people that Satan will NOT be deceiving during most of this future thousand-year age; an age when the glorified Christ is bodily on the earth and functioning as the King of kings and Lord of lords? They must be nations initially composed of righteous people since Christ declared in Matthew 13:36-43, that all the wicked will be put death at the end of this Gospel Age. In addition the Apostle Paul teaches that all righteous people will be given glorified bodies at Christ's Second Coming. This is when physical death comes to an end [I Corinthians 15:50-54]. Therefore, according to Christ and the Apostle Paul the only people on earth after Christ returns to raise the dead are righteous people in glorified bodies. And so I ask again, who are the people living on earth during a future thousand-year rule of the glorified Christ – in bodies that live longer but still die? Supposedly these people will continue to marry and have children –

many of whom will ultimately reject the glorified Christ according to Revelation 20:7-9.

A large number of Premillennialists try to solve the dilemma of people living on earth in flesh and blood bodies after Christ's Second Coming – by declaring a secret coming of Christ to raise the righteous dead and give Christians who are alive glorified bodies that will immediately be taken up into heaven. This secret coming of Christ will take place either seven, or three and a half years before Christ actually comes to the earth and sits on a throne at Jerusalem. The secret rapture of righteous people from the earth is when unbelieving Jewish people will get their eyes opened and turn to Christ as their Messiah. These believing Jews will then win converts to Christ all over the world for seven or three and a half years – while suffering great persecution by the Anti-Christ – until the Lord Jesus finally comes to the earth to begin His thousand-year rule. And when Christ actually comes to earth none of the people who become Christians at the end of this New Covenant Age will be given glorified bodies. According to the Dispensational viewpoint these are the righteous people in flesh and blood bodies who will enter into a thousand-year reign of the glorified Christ upon the earth – in fulfillment of Isaiah 65:20-23 [discussed in chapter 8].

However, the Apostle Paul provides another clear argument against a future thousand-year age after this New Covenant Age and before the Eternal State. Let's read I Corinthians 10:11,

"Now these things happened to them as an example [referring to the Jews who died in the wilderness because of their disobedience to God – Numbers 25:1-9], but they were written down for our instruction [New Covenant believers], on whom the ends of the ages has come."

Hebrews 9:26 also reads, "… he [Christ] has appeared once for all at the end of the ages to put away sin by the sacrifice of himself." Christ's death and resurrection is what inaugurated the New Covenant Age, which is the end of the ages. The Eternal State is what comes next.

In light of this information let's see if we can determine the beginning point of the thousand years spoken of in Revelation 20. Let me start by asking a question, "What is the key event in world history thus far?" Answer: The life, death, resurrection and ascension of Jesus Christ. The Incarnation is when God the Son became fully man without ceasing to be fully God. The angels are still talking about the wonder of that event. Listen to what Hebrews 2:14 teaches in regard to what happened to Satan at the cross,

"Since the children have flesh and blood, he too [God the Son] shared in their humanity so that by his death he might destroy him who holds the power of death – that is, the devil."

The Apostle Paul adds more details to Satan's defeat at the cross in Colossians 2:13-15 [ESV],

"And you, who were dead in your trespasses and the uncircumcision of your flesh, God made alive together with him [Christ], having forgiven us all our trespasses, 14by canceling the record of debt that stood against us with its legal demands. This [our debt against God] he set aside, nailing it to the cross. 15He disarmed the rulers and authorities [Satan and his demons] and put them to open shame, by triumphing over them in him."

If the thousand years of Revelation 20 begins at the cross, then there must be a binding of Satan at that time. Actually Jesus tells us in Matthew 12:28-29 that He had bound Satan even before the cross,

> "But if I [Jesus] drive out demons by the Spirit of God, then the kingdom of God has come upon you. [29]Or again, how can anyone enter a strong man's house and carry off his possessions unless he first binds [same word that is used in Revelation 20:2] the strong man? Then he can plunder his house."

The plundering of Satan's house continues every time someone is born again [Colossians 1:13-14]; which means our crucified and risen Lord Jesus has been plundering Satan's domain for almost two thousand years. And the primary people coming to Christ since the cross are the Gentiles, just as Revelation 20:3 declares. Because of what happened at the cross Satan is now less able to deceive people due to the new limitations [binding] placed upon him by Christ's death, resurrection and ascension to the Father's right hand.

Let's explore more about the meaning of Satan being chained and cast into the Abyss. What Jesus says in John 12:27-32 provides valuable insights,

> "Now is my heart troubled, and what shall I say? 'Father, save me from this hour' [the cross]? No, it was for this very reason I came ... [31]Now is the time for judgment on this world [the godless world system birthed by Satan]; now the prince of this world [Satan] will be cast out [same word as used in Revelation

20:3]. [32]But I, when I am lifted up from the earth [when I die on the cross], will draw all men to myself" [Jews and Gentiles].

There is a clear parallel between Revelation 20:1-3 and John 12:27-33. In what sense was Satan's power to deceive unbelievers diminished by Christ's death? At the cross God was made propitious toward rebellious mankind. To be made propitious means that instead of giving us the punishment we deserve, God can now justly give us the mercy and forgiveness we need. Satan cannot stop the power of the gospel, empowered by the Holy Spirit, from rescuing growing numbers of unbelievers from his domain of darkness and transferring them into Christ's kingdom of light. However, it is rightly said that Satan is like a mean dog bound to a length of chain. If a person walks into Satan's length of chain he will get chewed up. Unregenerated people are trapped and living within Satan's domain of darkness and are deceived and ensnared by his lies in varying degrees. Because there is still a large majority of people living in Satan's domain, blatant rebellion against God continues to happen. This is why many more people need to be transferred into Christ's kingdom of light and then taught by precept and example to stay on the path of life – which God has laid out for us in His moral law [see Psalm 119:35-37].

Let's look at Revelation 20:3 again,

"He [the angel of the Lord] threw [cast] him [Satan] into the Abyss, and locked and sealed it over him, to keep him from deceiving the nations [Gentiles] anymore until the thousand years were ended. After that, he must be set free for a short time."

Ironically the Abyss, or domain of darkness, is both Satan's kingdom and his prison. Revelation 9 speaks of a horde of demons being released upon people and reveals the identity of their leader in verse 11, "They had as a king over them the angel of the Abyss [Satan], whose name in Hebrew is Abaddon, and in Greek, Apollyon" [destroyer]. Jude 6 tells us something else about Satan and his demons,

> "And the angels who did not keep their positions of authority but abandoned their own home – these he has kept in darkness, bound with everlasting chains for judgment on the great Day."

All lost people are trapped, along with Satan and the demons, in the domain of darkness; a domain which gave birth to the world system, which is a way of thinking and behaving that is in opposition to God. However, at the cross Satan received a head wound which was an additional punishment heaped on top of being cast out of heaven and imprisoned on this spiritually darkened earth. Praise God for the growing outposts of light because of Christ's work on the cross. It is fitting that the location of the cross was at Golgatha, which means "place of the skull" – because it was there that Satan's skull was crushed or bruised in fulfillment of Genesis 3:15. But what is the meaning of Satan's brief release from the additional restraints placed upon him at the cross? I believe the end of the thousand years spoken of in Revelation 20:3, 4 and 7, is referring to the end of the New Covenant, Gospel Age. Revelation 20:7-9 discloses the effects of Satan's temporary discharge from his shackles,

"When the thousand years are over, Satan will be released from his prison [8]and will go out to deceive the nations in the four corners of the earth – Gog and Magog [generic terms for enemies of God] – to gather them for battle. In number they are like the sand on the seashore. [9]They marched across the breadth of the earth and surrounded the camp of God's people, the city he loves, but fire came down from heaven and devoured them."

Remember, according to the Premillennial view all these people became enemies of God while the glorified Christ was on the earth ruling over the nations – accompanied by billions of glorified saints. This brings up another problem for the Premillennial view. Hebrews 11:6 states, "And without faith it is impossible to please God, because anyone who comes to him must believe that he exists …" There will be no need of faith when people in flesh and blood bodies can see the glorified Christ and billions of glorified saints with their own eyes. And yet according to the Premillennial view even though glorious conditions will be enjoyed by all the peoples of the earth [in fulfillment of Isaiah 2:2-4; Isaiah 65:17-25], these enormously blessed followers of Christ will have children and grandchildren who grow up and decide that the glorified Christ is not worth following. And will also be convinced by Satan that they can defeat Him in battle. Really? Let's review the vision of the glorified Christ which the Apostle John saw in Revelation 1:12-18,

"I turned around to see the voice that was speaking to me. And when I turned I saw … someone 'like a son of man,' dressed in a robe reaching down to his feet and with a golden sash around his chest. [14]His head and hair were white like wool, as white as snow, and his eyes were like blazing fire. [15]His feet were like bronze glowing in a furnace, and his voice was like the sound of rushing waters. [16]In his right hand he held seven stars, and out of his mouth came a sharp double-edged sword. His face was like the sun shining in all its brilliance. [17]When I saw him, I fell at his feet as though dead. Then he placed his right hand on me and said: 'Do not be afraid. I am the First and the Last."

I personally do not think that people in flesh and blood bodies could actually see the glorified Christ and remain standing, let alone think they could defeat Him in battle. John merely saw a vision of the glorified Christ and thought he was going to die.

I should explain at this point that I believe Christ rose from the dead in the same body that hung on the cross, which is why He still had the nail prints in His hands and feet and a spear wound in His side. I am persuaded that it was when Christ was caught up into heaven [Luke 24:51-52; Acts 1:9] that He received His glorified body. In Acts 1:11 two angels said to the disciples as they watched Christ taken up into heaven,

> "Men of Galilee … why do you stand here looking into the sky? This same Jesus, who has been taken from you into heaven [in a glorified body suited for heaven], will come back in the same way you have seen him go into heaven" [in a glorified body].

I think that Christ's catching up into heaven serves as the blueprint for the rapture of Christians, which is when we get our glorified bodies – as foretold in I Corinthians 15:50-54. Most Christians believe Christ rose from the dead in His glorified body because He could walk into a room with locked doors and because people who knew Him did not initially recognize Him

[John 20:26-27; Luke 24:13-16]. But friends we must remember that when Christ was still in His flesh and blood body He walked on water [Matthew 14:25] and instantly calmed a storm [Mark 4:37-39]. We also have an account in Luke 4:29, when an angry crowd drove Jesus out of Nazareth and took him to a cliff in order to throw him down to his death. However, in verse 30 we read, "But he walked right through the crowd and went on his way." I do not think Christ had to have a glorified body in order to enter a room with locked doors or to change His appearance.

The reason I think this issue is worth examining is because I once spoke to a young man born with physical disabilities. He thought his crippled legs would be a part of his glorified body because Jesus still had nail prints and a spear wound in His glorified body. Do you agree with that young man? I don't.

Let's return to Revelation 20, while viewing the thousand years as referring to the New Covenant Age. Why will Satan be released from his restraints at the end of this Gospel Age? I believe the answer is given by our Lord Jesus in Matthew 13. Christ taught that the kingdom He began on earth [which all believers are a part of] is comparable to a farmer who planted good seeds in his field. However, an enemy [the devil] came along and sowed tares [pretend believers] among the good seeds. When the plants began to grow, the workers [mature believers in Christ] noticed that tares were mixed in with the wheat. They asked the owner [Christ] if He wanted them to pull the tares out? The owner said no, because in doing so they could harm the wheat. Jesus then explained that the tares will be separated from the wheat at the time of harvest. Listen to Christ's explanation of this parable in Matthew 13:39-41,

> "… the harvest is the end of the age [in this context Jesus is referring to the Gospel Age in which we live], and the harvesters are angels. [40]As the tares [unbelievers] are pulled up and burned with fire, so it will be at the end of the age. [41]The Son of Man will send out his angels, and they will weed out of his kingdom everything that causes sin and all who do evil."

Satan is an angel of God who has rebelled. Nevertheless, he is still under God's authority [Job 1:6-7]. At the end of this Gospel Age, Christ will remove His restraints upon Satan and have him gather up the tares. In this process of gathering the tares, these unbelievers will march against God's people. But the ascended Lord Jesus will dramatically intervene and put to death the warring unbelievers – and at the same time give His followers glorified bodies. This all happens at Christ's Second Coming. Revelation 20:4 is another verse we need to get right,

> "I saw thrones [in heaven] on which were seated those who had been given authority to judge. And I saw the souls of those who had been beheaded because of their testimony for Jesus and because of the word of God. They had not worshiped the beast or his image and had not received his mark on their foreheads or their hands. They came to life [they lived] and reigned with Christ a thousand years."

The "souls" that John saw in heaven can refer to people in resurrection bodies or to the spirits of believers who were killed for their faith in

Christ [absent from the body, present with the Lord – II Corinthians 5:6-8]. In the context of the book of Revelation, the souls would be martyred Christians who had not worshiped the beast [the Roman Empire – personified in its emperor Nero – Revelation 13:1-8, 18 – see previous chapter]. "They came to life" can also be translated "they lived". If John is saying "they came to life" – then this would support a bodily resurrection or a waking up from soul sleep. However, if John is saying "they lived" – then his statement agrees with the truth Jesus revealed to Martha in John 11:25-26,

> "I am the resurrection and the life. He who believes in me will live [same word as used in Revelation 20:4], even though he dies; [26] and whoever lives and believes in me will never die."

The Gospel of John is the only Gospel which records that conversation between Christ and Martha. I believe Revelation 20:4 is teaching that after John was banished to the Island of Patmos, he was given a vision into heaven. In this vision John was privileged to see the souls of believers who had been killed for their faith in Christ. John discovered in this vision that the words of Jesus to Martha were true, "He who believes in me will live, even though he dies." Nero could kill the bodies of believers but could not harm their souls [Matthew 10:28].

In Revelation 3:21 the ascended Lord Jesus gives us insight into the martyred saints reigning with Christ for a thousand years. Jesus spoke the following truth to the believers in the church at Laodicea, almost two thousand years ago,

> "To him who overcomes [remains faithful until death – I John 5:4], I will give the right to sit with me on my throne, just as I overcame and sat with my Father on his throne."

This promise indicates that departed saints are now ruling with Christ in heaven. I do not pray to departed saints, but neither do I think they are merely playing harps as they lounge around on clouds.

Here is another pertinent question. How can the thousand-year age of Revelation 20 refer to the New Covenant Age, since it has already been going for about two thousand years? In a book such as Revelation, we should not insist on a literal meaning for a thousand-year age. At times the Bible uses numbers in figurative ways. Listen to Psalm 50:9-10, "I (God) have no need of a bull from your stall or of goats from your pens, ¹⁰for every animal of the forest is mine, the cattle on a thousand hills." To press literalness on this passage would mean that God owns the cattle on a thousand hills, but no more than that. Of course we all know that God owns the cattle on all the hills – which amount to many more than a thousand.

The thousand years of Revelation 20 stand for a very long period of time. Through most of church history Christians have believed that the thousand years began at the cross and will end at Christ's final advent. This means that the believers John saw in heaven have been reigning with Christ for the past two thousand years.

It is worth contemplating that when unbelievers die they finally realize that Satan had duped them while they lived here on earth and is actually their mortal enemy. According to Luke 16:27-28, the unbelieving rich man who died and was being tormented in hades, wanted his living brothers to escape his fate. Unbelievers who die will no longer be duped by Satan and will certainly not serve him. In contrast, departed believers eagerly serve the One who gave His life so they could enter into eternal life. Unbelievers only serve Satan while they are on earth. Believers serve Christ while on earth and when they join Him in heaven.

Let's read Revelation 20:5-6 [ESV],

> "The rest of the dead did not come to life until the thousand years were ended. This is the first resurrection. ⁶Blessed and holy is the one who shares in the first resurrection! Over such the second death has no power, but they will be priests of God and of Christ, and they will reign with him for a thousand years."

Question: What is the "first resurrection" John refers to in Revelation 20:5? Let's answer that with another question: What is the first death that man experienced? It is alluded to in Genesis 2:17 [ESV], when God told Adam, "… of the tree of the knowledge of good and evil you shall not eat, for in the day that you eat of it you shall surely die." Did Adam and Eve die physically on the day they ate from that tree? No, they died spiritually [they lost their fellowship with God]. Many years later they also died physically. The first death that people must overcome – is spiritual death. The first resurrection people must experience in order to overcome spiritual death – is spiritual resurrection, which takes place at the time of regeneration [Colossians 2:13]. All the people John saw alive in heaven had experienced the first resurrection – regeneration in Christ. The great bodily resurrection will not occur until the final advent of Christ, which coincides with the end of the thousand years spoken of in

Revelation 20:5, "The rest of the dead [unbelievers who have not been spiritually born again] did not come to life until the thousand years were ended."

When a Christian is living on earth he or she enjoys fellowship with the Father, Son and Holy Spirit. At the moment a Christian physically dies his or her spirit immediately goes to heaven and enjoys even greater fellowship with our Triune God. In other words, Christians experience no separation or breaking of fellowship with God at the time of physical death [Romans 8:38-39]. On the other hand an unbeliever is physically alive but spiritually dead while on earth. At the time of physical death an unbeliever's spirit continues to be separated from God in hades. The only taste of real life that unbelievers will experience is when they are bodily resurrected and stand in God's presence. Philippians 2:10-11 declares that at that time every knee shall bow and every tongue confess that Jesus is Lord to the glory of God the Father. But at the great bodily resurrection, even after unbelievers make the admission that Jesus is Lord, they will still hear the words, "Depart from me you who practice lawlessness" [Matthew 7:23]. At the Great White Throne Judgement of Revelation 20:11, all resurrected unbelievers will suffer eternal separation from God in the lake of fire [Revelation 20:14-15]. This is the second death spoken of in Revelation 20:6.

Important note: The Premillennial view teaches that there will be two bodily resurrections – one for believers at Christ's Second Coming and a separate bodily resurrection for unbelievers a thousand years later. This viewpoint conflicts with what Jesus taught in John 5:28-29 [NASB],

> "Do not marvel at this; for an hour is coming, in which all who are in the tombs shall hear his voice, [29]and come forth; those who did the good deeds, to a resurrection of life, those who committed the evil deeds to a resurrection of judgment."

Do you see a thousand years between the resurrection of the righteous and the resurrection of the unrighteous in those verses? Neither do I.

In Revelation 20:9, I believe the city God loves is either a reference to the Church in general [Galatians 4:25-26] or specifically to the city of Jerusalem, whose Jewish inhabitants are destined to come into the blessings of the New Covenant through faith in Christ [Jeremiah 31:33-34; Romans 11:11-12]. The reason unbelievers will march against believers is because Christians will have possessed the gate of our enemies by this time [Genesis 22:16-18], which is why I believe there will be many more believers than unbelievers at the close of this New Covenant Age. So why don't we read anything about Christians taking up arms to defend themselves against this end of the age horde of unbelievers? We will understand by looking at one of the blessings destined to spread to all the nations because of the New Covenant, which Christ inaugurated during the last days of the Old Covenant Age [Hebrews 1:1-2; Hebrews 8:13]. This blessing is spoken of in Micah 4:1-3, which is a clear description of a successful Great Commission,

> "In the last days [of the Old Covenant Age in which the prophet Micah lived] the mountain [kingdom] of the LORD's temple [the Church] will be established as chief among the mountains [earthly kingdoms]; it will be raised [this speaks of a process]

above the hills, and peoples will stream to it. ²Many nations will come and say, 'Come, let us go up to the mountain of the LORD, to the house of the God of Jacob [Christ's kingdom is the most desirable of all kingdoms because there is no better king to rule over us than King Jesus, and there are no better laws to live by than God's law]. He [Christ] will teach us his ways, so that we may walk in his paths.' The law will go out from Zion, the word of the LORD from Jerusalem [Jesus commanded His disciples to stay in Jerusalem until the Holy Spirit was poured out. Since Acts 2 the temple of God and kingdom of Christ have spread from Jerusalem into all the nations]. ³He will judge between many peoples and will settle disputes for strong nations far and wide [as the Church makes disciples of the nations]. They [the nations] will beat their swords into plowshares and their spears into pruning hooks. Nation will not take up sword against nation, nor will they train for war anymore."

A successful Great Commission will bring about a depth of peace which no longer requires weapons of war. Notice in verse 2 that the law will go out from Zion. Just as the good news of the gospel was to go out from Jerusalem into all the nations, so was God's law. Why is that important? Because God's law is the standard of right and wrong. It is when all the nations can agree upon the same standard of right and wrong that the ascended Lord Jesus will settle disputes for strong nations far and wide. Churches that neglect to teach the benefits of God's law, are failing to educate Christians on one of the specific elements of God's Word that will enable nations to settle disputes without resorting to war.

Let's now return to Revelation 20:9-10. I believe Christ's Church will not have to defend itself from the attack by unbelievers at the end of this New Covenant Age – because the Lord Jesus will deliver His people by means of His long awaited Second Coming. It is at this time when Satan and all the demons are cast into the lake of fire, along with all unbelievers who will follow them into that abode.

Here is an important question. What will prompt Christ to release Satan from his present bindings and bring the New Covenant Age to a close? It will happen when God is able to say, "I have now fulfilled all the promises I made to Abraham's descendants and to the peoples of the earth." Future unbelievers living at the end of this New Covenant Age, will experience the blessings of long life-spans and a depth of peace which enables the nations to beat their swords into plowshares – and yet they will stubbornly choose to reject Christ. This means they will have reached a hardness of heart that prevents them from repenting of their sins and placing their trust in the person and work of the Lord Jesus. The judgment described in Revelation 20:9-10, will occur at the end of this New Covenant Age. The judgment that was near at hand when John wrote the book of Revelation is what closed out the Old Covenant Age in A.D. 70.

If indeed the New Covenant Age is the end of the ages, then the great blessings promised by God to Abraham's descendants and to the nations of the world – must be fulfilled during this New Covenant Age. Dr. David Snoke, a professor in the department of physics and astronomy at the University of Pittsburgh and an ordained elder in the Presbyterian Church of America, wrote the following,

"Decay is a result of the second law of thermodynamics, which states that disorder always increases, that is, everything must run down eventually ... time runs forward and not backward because of the second law of thermodynamics. This is a deep point of physics not always appreciated by non-experts. We can only tell the passage of time with a "clock," a natural cycle. But we cannot tell whether the cycle is running forward or backward unless there is decay. Thus the abolishment of decay literally means the end of time."

Christ's coming to raise the dead and give believers glorified bodies that never die is referred to as the "last day" [John 6:39-40]. Why? Because it ushers in the Eternal State, when time will be no more.

Let me finish by asking this question: Do you know Christ in a saving way? That is only possible by confessing that we have sinned and fallen short of God's standards of right and wrong. But because God sent His one and only Son into this world to willingly take our sins upon Himself, and fully bear the Father's wrath against those sins, we can now be forgiven and made clean by Christ's imputed righteousness to our accounts. Friends, the worst of sinners are not beyond the grace of God.

Scriptures referred to but not quoted:

Psalm 119:35-36, "Direct me in the path of your commands, for there I find delight. ³⁶Turn my heart toward your statutes and not toward selfish gain."

Genesis 3:15, "And I will put enmity between you [Satan] and the woman [Eve], and between your offspring and hers; he [Eve's most important offspring] will crush your head, and you will strike his heel."

Luke 24:51-52, "While he was blessing them, he left them and was taken up into heaven. ⁵²Then they worshiped him and returned to Jerusalem with great joy."

Acts 1:9, "After he said this, he was taken up before their very eyes, and a cloud hid him from their sight."

This was foretold in Daniel 7:13-14. I am going to actually let you look those verses up yourself.

John 20:26-27, "A week later his disciples were in the house again, and Thomas was with them. Though the doors were locked, Jesus came and stood among them and said, "Peace be with you!" ²⁷Then he said to Thomas, 'Put your finger here; see my hands. Reach out your hand and put it into my side. Stop doubting and believe."

Luke 24:13-16, "Now that same day two of them were going to a village called Emmaus, about seven miles from Jerusalem. ¹⁴They were talking with each other about everything that had happened. ¹⁵As they talked and discussed these things with each other, Jesus himself came up and walked along with them; ¹⁶but they were kept from recognizing him."

Matthew 14:25, "During the fourth watch of the night Jesus went out to them, walking on the lake."

Mark 4:37-39, "A furious squall came up, and the waves broke over the boat, so that it was nearly swamped ... He got up, rebuked the wind and said to the waves, 'Quiet! Be still!' Then the wind died down and it was completely calm."

Job 1:6-7, "One day the angels came to present themselves before the LORD, and Satan also came with them. [7]The LORD said to Satan, 'Where have you come from?' Satan answered the LORD, 'From roaming through the earth and going back and forth in it."

II Corinthians 5:6-8, "Therefore we are always confident and know that as long as we are at home in the body we are away from the Lord ... [8]We are confident, I say, and would prefer to be away from the body and at home with the Lord."

Matthew 10:28, "Do not be afraid of those who kill the body but cannot kill the soul. Rather, be afraid of the One who can destroy both soul and body in hell."

I John 5:4, "for everyone born of God overcomes the world."

Colossians 2:13, "When you were dead in your sins and in the uncircumcision of your sinful nature, God made you alive with Christ."

Romans 8:38-39, "For I am convinced that neither death nor life, neither angels nor demons, neither the present nor the future, nor any powers, [39]neither height nor depth, nor anything else in all creation, will be able to separate us from the love of God that is in Christ Jesus our Lord."

Galatians 4:25-26, "Now Hagar stands for Mount Sinai in Arabia and corresponds to the present city of Jerusalem, because she is in slavery with her children. ²⁶But the Jerusalem that is above is free, and she is our mother."

Hebrews 1:1-2, "In the past God spoke to our forefathers through the prophets at many times and in various ways, ² but in these last days [of the Old Covenant Age] he has spoken to us by his Son, whom he appointed heir of all things, and through whom he made the universe."

Hebrews 8:13, "By calling this covenant "new," [speaking of the New Covenant inaugurated by Christ's death and resurrection] he has made the first one [the Old Covenant] obsolete; and what is obsolete and aging will soon disappear." A few years later the temple was destroyed, which marked the official end of Old Covenant Israel and the Old Covenant Age.

John 6:39-40, "And this is the will of him who sent me, that I shall lose none of all that he has given me, but raise them up at the last day. ⁴⁰For my Father's will is that everyone who looks to the Son and believes in him shall have eternal life, and I will raise him up at the last day."